On Decency

On Decency

The CORTHODOX Way

A. E. SMITH

WIPF & STOCK • Eugene, Oregon

ON DECENCY
The CORTHODOX Way

Wipf & Stock
An Imprint of Wipf and Stock Publishers
199 W. 8th Ave., Suite 3
Eugene, OR 97401

www.wipfandstock.com

PAPERBACK ISBN: 979-8-3852-6300-4
HARDCOVER ISBN: 979-8-3852-6301-1
EBOOK ISBN: 979-8-3852-6302-8

03/04/26

Contents

Introduction

The CORTHODOX Way

Dear Reader,

Family, educators, and religious leaders have taught most of us how to behave well and interact successfully with other people. Modern individuals who live in free societies often reject "sets" of ideas developed by well-meaning people. When the "shoe does not fit," we borrow this and that from a variety of traditions, eras, and people we admire. We create our personal list of "never do that," "sometimes do this," and "well, that's not really a big no-no."

This practice means that many of us have formed an ineffective hard-to-remember set of personal values. It also means that our society lacks a practical, common, predictable set of normative behaviors. When we do our own "I-centered" thing, it tears at the strength of the familial, social, and political fabric of society. Since no consensus ties us together, we sometimes develop a disdain for each other. Distrust and disunity can develop. Society may fragment into tribe-like factions of people who "think" alike.

A new synthesis of memorable guidelines respectfully drawn from multiple sources could provide a set of basic values that would unite rather than divide us.

The world is home to billions of diverse people. The US is home to one of the most diverse populations on earth. Although it was underpopulated for a long time, people were encouraged to come here and help us build the country we have today. The melting pot of people who call the United States home is both a blessing and a challenge, and one of the reasons Americans have no established religion, no single set of broadly accepted values, and no basic unifying moral code that we all can agree to share.

What if we could share a set of decency norms that would unite us *and* maintain our diversity?

Some people would prefer to impose their religious values on others, but the outcome of doing so would be unconstitutional and create even more division. Perhaps some of the stress and strain between diverse groups would soften if people everywhere embraced the decency values described here. Might the US, a diverse country, be an example to people in other countries who live with internal differences and conflict caused by diversity? Could the decency values of the CORTHODOX Way soften the harsh edges of the various cultures and beliefs that exist on what feels like a smaller planet?

In short, the Corthodox Way is meant to address the "values chaos" problem. Nine fundamental values are linked to a mnemonic device that spells the word CORTHODOX. My hope is that this simple, memorable set of nine values can serve individuals well and help our diverse society, and perhaps societies around the world, to become more unified in our expectations of each other.

CORTHODOX values are drawn from multiple sources, secular and religious. The value system is not intended to replace or compete with your faith tradition if you have one. CORTHODOX values are not intended to lead you to spiritual insight or a stronger relationship with the divine. Various faith traditions have this as their purpose. While the values discussed here overlap or reinforce many religious values, the CORTHODOX Way does not belong to any one philosophical, theological, or religious tradition. It belongs to all of them and all of us. The CORTHODOX Way helps unite us around a value system that promotes the practice of decency virtues, despite the rural/urban divide and the faith-centered/secular divide that characterizes modern societies.

Some social critics and people who fear the decline of Christianity among the secular-minded people of our era argue that religion has always played a *necessary* moral role. They are afraid that the modern, individualistic mindset has undercut moral norms because freedom-loving people no longer want to submit to a higher authority or rules and practices fashioned in other eras, often by men with some form of authority that was not to be questioned.

Fearful of the secularists, some of the religious people in our society want the government to play a part in imposing or promoting *at least some* basic religious values, for the sake of social stability.[1] Some American conservatives are consulting leaders in Hungary and Poland, both predominately Catholic countries, to see if they can glean a way forward. That shoe will never fit countries with diverse populations and traditions. Freedom-loving people, male and female, are unlikely to embrace historic cultural norms passed down by political and religious authority figures from much earlier eras. Besides, the horse has left the barn, as they say, and recognizing reality is more helpful than trying to turn the clock back by way of repression.

Nevertheless, we do need a degree of common ethical ground if we are to fare well individually and socially. A frayed society becomes a tribal society, and tribal societies are divided and weak. Nation-states require a degree of social cohesion. We need a plumb line of decency values that can be widely embraced. My sources are varied; they are both secular and religious, ancient and modern. And yet, as the quotes at the end of each chapter indicate, the CORTHODOX values are supported by a wide variety of people from various eras and traditions. I am an intellectual historian who has an interest in how "values" change over time, sometimes slowly, sometimes fast and furiously. Social and intellectual norms do not remain static.

I do not think that the unchurched, a.k.a. the "nones," are unethical because their values are not underpinned by religious authority.[2] Consider the pre-Christian era in the Mediterranean world. Were the ancient Greece and Romans bereft of values? Hardly. Greek philosophers "wrote the book" on ethics. They relied on reason to deliberate on what is ethical and "good." In other words, they examined the *outcomes* of certain actions and labeled some actions "good" and other actions "bad." According to the historian Thucydides, history is the final judge, and consequences are the evidence.[3]

1. See Schwartz, "Advocate."

2. More than 20 percent of the US population identify as "nones." About 40 percent of millennials are "nones." The nonreligious, the skeptics, agnostics, atheists, and secular humanists among us are well represented by Greg Epstein, author of *Good Without God*. Jacqui Lewis argues that if humankind is to thrive, we need to let go of any religion that wounds and kills. She says that some of what we believe about God is about us, that we create God in our own image. That means some of us imagine *God* to be punitive, angry, and vengeful (*Courage and Rule-Breaking Kindness*, 129–30, 193–94).

3. Some people talk about being on the "right side" of history. But "history" is not meant to judge us like a deity of some sort. We make history. We craft it, interpret it, learn from it, and protect it—*if* we are free to analyze, criticize, and draw from the full story. One of the first acts of Communist regimes and other forms of tyranny is to rewrite

To the four virtues that the Greeks identified as in harmony with reason and nature, *wisdom, justice, courage, and temperance*, early Catholic Church leaders added the three theological virtues, *faith, hope, and love.* Thus, the seven cardinal (a.k.a. *hinge*) virtues were defined and developed. They were/are regarded as basic and necessary for a moral life and the good of society. Early Christians leaned on their cultural predecessors, so ideas about the "virtues" come to us from multiple sources, including reason and revelation, philosophy and theology, trial and error, and history.

Philosophers like Immanuel Kant (d. 1804), a Prussian intellectual, used rational analysis to develop a list of virtues known as *categorical imperatives.*[4] These virtues include *self-respect, honesty, thrift, self-improvement, beneficence, gratitude, sociability, and forgiveness.* The term *categorical imperatives* means that these are essential virtues, because to ignore them is destructive, irrational, and chaotic. To discern whether you should act in a certain way, Kant proposes that you ponder whether other people and society would benefit if *everyone acted the way you are considering acting.* Practice is important, Kant said, because immoral behavior can, over time, become normative and common. When that happens, society becomes coarse, crude, and more likely to disintegrate as a variety of groups become alienated from each other. It would be wise to avoid that.

None of the earlier lists of virtues address the "I-centeredness" that emerged in the 1960s, mostly in the West. As "we-centeredness" declined, a splintering of society followed. Frankly, society has not benefitted from each of us doing our own thing. A frayed fabric of social norms now exists. This splintering needs to be repaired, but without a heavy-handed approach and with respect for individuals of all sorts.

How do we get all the diverse people who make up our national family (and the world as well?) to share moral values that will strengthen the fabric of society and the common good? My academic background and interests have led me to develop a list of the characteristics that I hope will have wide personal appeal and, by extension, social usefulness.

My graduate studies focused on the history of ideas. Ideas emerge, die or flourish, and are integrated and modified over time. Ideas are powerful.

history, to bend it to tell the story they want to tell.

4. For example, if you heartily promise that you *will repay* a loan to convince someone to advance you some money, while *knowing* you are unlikely to be able to repay the loan, that behavior would lack virtue, because the maxim this behavior would set is this: *If you can benefit from making a false promise, you should.* The world would not work better if everyone acted like this. Trust would decline; interest rates would go up.

As a college educator and historian, I have taught western and world history, as well as world regional geography and leadership classes. I have a passing knowledge of the mainstream world religions and the wide variety of cultural norms. Thucydides, an ancient Greek historian, suggested that while the first purpose of historians is to objectively tell historical stories, historians should also *use* those stories to observe the causes and consequences of beliefs and actions taken. What works, what undermines, what unifies, what strengthens, what destroys, and what divides. In short, history can play a role in identifying pragmatic, positive values. Like the Greeks, I, too, think studying history can be a lesson in the consequences of embracing certain ideas and monitoring the outcomes.

Beneath the main historical story lie lessons to be learned, behaviors to be admired and emulated, and reasons to avoid behaviors that result in tragedy or chaos. Historical stories that condense time, and the actions, motives, and decisions of major players and "the people" can reveal a clearer picture of what works well and what does not work well. The present is always blurry. We are too close to it, and the story has yet to unfold as to the consequences of actions taken.

In each chapter I have used the ideas and teachings of a variety of people, respected historical figures as well as contemporary observers. I have gleaned from many admirable people to show that the ideas presented here come not only from me but also from the writings of a lot of "good company." What I own as original is this compilation. I propose that the adoption and practice of CORTHODOX values will have a positive effect on both individuals and the larger society.

Historians must be professional writers of history; they must follow the strict discipline of the profession. Otherwise, we are "using" history inappropriately. Even so, observing the consequences of values and actions need not distort the usefulness of the objectively written story. Care is nevertheless essential, for how history is written and taught has consequences, hence the controversy over the 1619 Project and the debate over how history should be taught to pre-college-age students.[5]

Never forget that in the post–World War II era the countries that became Communist wanted to control the minds of young students, so history was rewritten so that Marxist ideology could take root in a favorable way. History should never be the tool of ideology, any ideology. Too much

5. See PBS *News Hour*, "1619 Project"; and 1619 Project.

is lost; too much is distorted. Ideology is for lazy people willing to join a parade to an unknown place. Truth seekers avoid such parades.

As an intellectual historian, I observe and trace how and why ideas survive, thrive, are modified, or die. From the long view, Western civilization has been shaped by two grand eras that form the yin and the yang of Western culture: 1) the Greco-Roman or classical period (800 BCE—470 CE) and 2) the Judeo-Christian tradition that formed in the ancient world of Southwest Asia, was adopted and modified in the late Roman Empire (300–500 CE), and was then passed on throughout the Middle Ages (500–1450 CE) and into the modern era. These two traditions form the backbone of Western civilization.[6] The push and pull of these two consequential periods has always fascinated me and been part of my academic research. In terms of ethical values, these two traditions overlap and even merge in certain eras (the Italian Renaissance, for example), but they are not often in complete alignment.

The reason-vs.-faith conflicts in Western history and strains of anti-intellectualism can be seen in the execution of Socrates (399 BCE). Socrates was executed for corrupting the youth and disrespecting the gods. Cicero (43 BCE) was executed for his political and cosmopolitan positions. His head and hands were hacked off. In the seventeenth century CE Galileo was silenced and placed under house arrest for suggesting that our system was sun centered (solar system), not geocentric as the church taught. In Islam, the Mu'tazila school of thought of the ninth century embraced rationalism and intellectual inquiry in the Islamic world. Suppression led to a decline in intellectual inquiry and a shift toward faith over reason. Martin Luther, who held a doctorate in theology, insisted that the role of reason and intellectualism in religious study be abandoned for "faith alone." The Enlightenment or the "age of reason" in seventeenth- and eighteenth-century Europe gave us John Locke, Thomas Jefferson, Voltaire, and Kant, but a reactionary period (Romanticism) followed the Enlightenment era. Traditionalists

6. Some people have argued that East and West will never meet, that the Western experience of a democratic Greece and a republican Rome that embraced Christianity renders the West distinct from other regions and cultures that were shaped by other faith traditions and various forms of royals and emperors, or top-down rulers and elites. Yet blending is a trait of the modern era. Japan is certainly an example of an Asian culture that adopted Western norms while also maintaining cultural values with ancient roots. Religious diversity there is not a big source of division. Various philosophies and religions, including the Shinto tradition, Buddhism, and Christianity somehow come together. As people move more freely around the world, Japan can serve as a model of tolerance and assimilation.

viewed the "enlightened rationalists" with suspicion, especially after the upheaval of the French and American Revolutions.

The fascism of Hitler and Mussolini was anti-intellectual, racist, and authoritarian. The Jews were known to be well educated and successful, making them dangerous radicals. Jewish, socialist, and liberal authors were held in disdain, and their books were burned in 1933. Universities were purged of dissenting scholars, and research was constrained.

The historical pattern is this: Suspicion of intellectuals rises in reaction to social or political upheaval, especially when the people who have traditionally had power feel threatened by ideas that buck the status quo.[7] In the US, we had the Scopes Monkey Trial of 1925, McCarthyism in the 1950s, the rise of the religious right in the 1970s. At the beginning of this century, we have had populist movements like the Tea Party, and grassroots challenges to intellectuals and scientists who gave us vaccines and safe milk. The populists in the US distrust science or see it as antithetical to their faith tradition or to their social and/or religious values. Social media platforms deliver falsehoods, half-truths, and disinformation by way of unregulated platforms. Ironically, the people who know the least think they are "in the know."

Western people have managed to blend reason and revelation. Like most people in the West, I have been influenced by the "dos and don'ts" that come from the blending of the ideas and values of the classical era and the Judeo-Christian era. These include the Ten Commandments of the Old Testament and the seven cardinal virtues, which include the four classical virtues (*prudence, justice, fortitude, and temperance*) and the three theological virtues (*faith, hope and love*).[8] These seven cardinal virtues are accepted by the mainline Western churches today, including the Roman Catholic, Episcopal, Lutheran, and Methodist Churches. Knowledge of these virtues helps people form a disposition to be good and to do good, and it blends classical and Christian values.

In his book *Embracing the Kingdom,* Kenneth Swanson lists and describes ten sins in an updated version of the traditional list of the seven sins codified by Pope Gregory the Great (d. 604). The ten sins he discusses are: pride, greed, gluttony, lust, envy, sloth, anger, dishonesty, fear, and despair. The virtues he lists are humility, faith, hope, agape (unconditional love), apatheia (the inner freedom that frees us from compulsion), peace, kindness,

7. See Paine, "Intellectual Divide."

8. Colón, "Seven Heavenly Virtues."

generosity, purity of heart, *hupomone* (patience, steadfastness), and wisdom. This is a helpful read and includes a prayer discipline for embracing the virtues he describes.[9]

I like pondering the ideal virtues of an era and the consequences of people adopting and implementing them. Questions come up easily. For example, can something be virtuous for women but not for men? Does a true virtue have universality?[10] My conclusion is that cultural norms are not necessarily virtues. Virtues are built around what people value in others over a prolonged period. Virtues are the traits you want your family and friends to have; all of them apply to both males and females. The CORTHODOX Way embraces the virtues that have staying power, i.e., good consequences. Lists of dos and don'ts can easily fade from memory, especially the "don'ts." (Nine of the Ten Commandments tell you what to *abstain* from doing, so the commandments are only indirectly a list of virtues.)

Christianity threw a wrench in the norms of Jews and pagans alike by talking less about the "rules" of tradition and propriety and more about charity, kindness, and forgiveness, a way of seeing and being in the world, i.e., an alternate consciousness. No new list of virtues emerges from Jesus's teachings. Jesus offered up the Golden Rule and the Great Commandment,[11] which require a generous/forgiving point of view and an awareness that God (Divine Mind) is a unifier. These are the rules of a rule breaker and a generous liberator. Jesus had a more heart-centered/mystical approach

9. Swanson, *Enter the Kingdom*, 147–55.

10. Voltaire said, "Virtue is everywhere the same, because it comes from God, while everything else is of man" (Bradley et al., *International Dictionary of Thoughts*, 756).

11. The Golden Rule is to treat others as you would like to be treated (Matt 7:12; Luke 6:31). The Great Commandment is to "love the Lord your God with all your heart and with all your soul and with all your mind and with all your strength." Jesus's commandment steps it up a notch and goes beyond altruism. Keeping this commandment requires the ability to see all of God's people, and creation, as unified and sacred. "The second is this: You shall love your neighbor as yourself. There is no other commandment greater than these" (Mark 12:28–31).

Some Buddhists (Lao-tzu) and Christian mystics (Julian of Norwich and St. Francis of Assisi), as well as Wang Yang-Ming (Neo-Confucian) of the late fifteenth and early sixteenth century, appear to have reached this awareness. They all strived to live by the Great Commandment. Most of us have only glimpses of the unity of creation and the love of the Creator that binds it all together. A writer who succinctly and poetically describes the connectivity of the particular with the universal and the eternal is Anthony De Mello: "The sun and its light, the ocean and the wave, the singer and his song—not one, not two" (*One Minute Wisdom*, 31).

than a rule-centered approach.[12] (Yet he could analyze, debate, and argue with experienced Jewish scholars from a young age.)

Christians believe that God is love and that love unites all people and creation. Against the assertion that God is a "just" God, Christians like Paul, a Roman citizen and a well-educated Jew, tell us that God is a generous God, the God of everyone.[13] The idea that *all of God's people have dignity* is rooted in both Stoicism and Christianity. This idea is no small matter. The human rights movement emerges from the soil of these two *Western* traditions.

Religious leaders who emphasized that people please God by being the keepers of rules were horrified by some of the rules/laws/norms that Jesus flouted. He seemed to live with reckless abandon! He healed on the Sabbath. He dined with tax collectors and prostitutes. He told parables about extravagant generosity and praised a woman who broke open a costly alabaster jar to anoint him with precious oil. Jesus was a compelling leader and a worthy role model, but a rule maker he was not. He went straight to the heart of people, offering a new way of seeing and thinking, and his metaphor for this new consciousness was "the kingdom of God."

The lists mentioned earlier, the seven cardinal virtues and the Ten Commandments, can be hard to recall, and the language seems to belong to another era, even if the virtues themselves are timeless. Modern secularists and "nones" are unlikely to embrace and live by a traditional list of religious virtues, and their numbers are growing, not declining. The chapters in this text explore values from various traditions, some religious, some not. What I am offering is a precise, functional identification of the basic values of human decency.

The values discussed here are pragmatic and timely. I am optimistic that this text could make a difference and create some common ground for people who have a variety of beliefs and ideas. By outlining the characteristics of basic decency, I hope to direct human behavior to positive outcomes

12. The tension between mysticism and morality is one of the three major dilemmas in religious thought. The two summary commandments described above are easy to remember, and they are a useful summary of what Jesus said that *really* matters. Jesus's primary audience was made up of Jews who were trying to navigate a multiplicity of laws and traditions that had formed layer after layer of "dos and don'ts" over an extended period of time.

13. Once summarized as follows: "We hold these truths to be self-evident . . . that all men are created equal, that they are endowed by their Creator with certain unalienable Rights, that among these are Life, Liberty, and the Pursuit of Happiness" (Declaration of Independence, 1776).

and to help us increase and rebuild a useful, pragmatic consensus and community. Even though we are politically, culturally, and ideologically distinct in many ways, perhaps we can see the benefit of uniting around a common way of being, becoming, and interacting.

The decency values of CORTHODOX are universally applicable and mnemonically memorable. They belong to no single culture or tradition. They are drawn from philosophy, faith traditions, history, and admirable individuals. They are pragmatic and useful; they have a good historical track record.

Intellectual historians trace the consequences of certain ideas through time; they have an exceedingly long view. I admire and use the ideas of great thinkers. I have selected from a rich heritage of ideas. I have my favorites. I like Aristotle's pragmatism. Aristotle explored the "nature" of humanity and our highest purposes or "virtues." I deeply appreciate the Stoic tradition from which we get our ideas about human dignity, tranquility, equality, human rights, and the laws that protect our "divinely given" rights. Stoicism is a wonderful guide to living with simplicity and without anxiety. It is helpful in interpersonal values, i.e., how to respect and treat each other.[14] (I hope it makes a comeback of sorts.) I am a long-time Christian, in part because of my family's influence, also because I find Jesus's behavior and teachings uniquely fascinating. As you read this you will see that I have pieced together the traits of the CORTHODOX Way. I simply want to say that you will see that I am indebted to various traditions and have pieced together a colorful quilt of ideas that are meant to be helpful to a broad base of people who want to be, at the very least, decent. This is not an academic work; it is a conversation between me and my readers. In my attempt to unite and inspire people of this era, I took the liberty of looking in a wide variety of places.

In summary, ours is a harsh, fragmented, but connected world. This treatise was written because I saw a need in our society, and in the world, for basic common decency values that foster reliability, kindness, and trust. If the behaviors described here become broadly used standards of common practice, we would have far more common ground than we do now. CORTHODOX decency values do not require uniformity of religious beliefs, nor do they offer rewards in the afterlife. They are drawn from mainstream sources and a variety of traditions as the basis for common practices.

14. I highly recommend William Irvine, *A Guide to the Good Life*. This little book is calming, enlightening, accessible (easy to read), and empowering.

I hope CORTHODOX moves beyond the Western world; it may or may not. (Much of the non-Western world makes a habit of attacking Westerners because of the imperialistic era.) As a Westerner, perhaps I will be dismissed too. I hope not, because I think that basic decency should be universal, and I have purposely selected people from a variety of cultural traditions.

I started my journey on this path with a provocative question I read in an article by David Brooks. Brooks asked: "Does America still have a moral core, a basic framework that makes this a decent place to live?"[15] My first thought when I read that was "not really, but I could help with that." So, I set out to provide a basic guide for this era using what I have learned from other eras.[16] I think that people of varying traditions can use this decency code *and* expect their leaders and fellow citizens to live in accordance with these values as well.

Naturally, a list of "decent" behaviors has the effect of identifying indecent behaviors (just as a list of the seven virtues naturally leads to a list of the seven deadly sins). Should CORTHODOX be used to hold people, ideologies, movements, and institutions (even religious ones) accountable? Frankly, I hope that *is* the case, because it is clear to me that the consequences of "anything goes" are too negative. Too many people in our society arrogantly violate, ignore, dismiss, and undermine the rules of basic decency; that is a raw deal, for them and for the rest of us. Behavior has consequences, large and small. I see a real need for common clear values that could become normative and belong to all of us.

Since the CORTHODOX Way has no formal enforcement mechanism, people must speak up for and defend the rules of basic decency by

15. D. Brooks, "At His Core," para. 11.

16. My academic research relates to how Renaissance scholars revived classical values. They challenged the medieval *ideal* of "virtue," which was the religious life (a.k.a. the contemplative life), the life of monks and nuns who retreated from the City of Man in search of the City of God. Virtue is not the same in every era. When the virtues of one era give way to the virtues of another era, there is a great deal of push and pull. For example, racism was once the common sense of an era, and laws were passed enforcing segregation. Now we judge racism harshly. The virtues of nationalism and national identity evolved later than you might think, after nation-states formed in the late medieval/early modern era. Over time martyrdom shifted. Whereas medieval people highly valued dying for God and the faith, the idea of dying for one's country had yet to inspire patriotic martyrdom, until the modern era of nation-states. Renaissance Florence, a republic, had humanist scholars who revived Greek and Roman traditions that defined "the good life" and ideas about fighting for one's homeland. In fourteenth and fifteenth-century Florence, fighting for freedom and against tyranny revived the idea of patriotic martyrdom.

denouncing rather than ignoring indecency. People must be called out for indecent behavior, in a supportive sort of way, because human society is better for it. When we call out indecent *behaviors*, we are reinforcing decency values, but we are not condemning *people*. We are playing a part in upholding decency norms, i.e., the desired behaviors that civilize and unify, particularly in democratic countries with rule of law and free speech protections. We have some good examples of people pushing against indecent behaviors, especially liars. This has been done before.[17]

Secular and religious leaders are imperfect individuals who will sometimes violate CORTHODOX ideals; we all do. But leaders take on the responsibility of being role models for numerous people, so their behavior matters even more. Since this is the case, we must hold leaders to higher standards. Sincere apologies are to be considered, and forgiveness plays a necessary role in human decency. And yet, the people in leadership positions must adhere to the basic standards of decency, for they are, like it or not, setting an example. The violation of basic decency norms is not to be accepted as normal practice in any institution, secular or religious, even though we all violate decency values on occasion.

When you know the core values of the CORTHODOX Way, you will also know many of the traits of true leaders. You will have a plumb line for deciding who is worthy of having you as a follower and who is not. You may even acquire the confidence to be a leader yourself. At the very least, you will not live a rudderless life.

Because CORTHODOX values are not rooted in any specific tradition, philosophy, or ideology, the values or norms described in this treatise can serve as a useful, practical way *to evaluate* the basic decency of ideas and policies, the actions of people, the function of institutions, and the usefulness or harm of emerging ideas and movements. Protecting basic decency is unifying and essential; it is the work of all of us. Kant was right

17. One of the most iconic lines in modern American political history occurred in 1954 during the Cold War and the Red Scare. Senator Joe McCarthy used the fear of Communism to gain fame as an adamant anti-Communist. He accused and undermined fellow senators, university professors, members of the UN, and numerous others, using a new invention, television. It was useful to McCarthy, who was ambitious and eager for national fame, until Joseph N. Welch, a Boston lawyer, challenged him after McCarthy asserted that Communists had infiltrated the US Army. A single question in front of eighty million viewers led to McCarthy's demise. Welch pointedly asked McCarthy this question: "Until this moment, Senator, I think I have never really gauged your cruelty or your recklessness. . . . Have you no sense of *decency*[,] sir, at long last? Have you left no sense of *decency*?" (American Rhetoric, "McCarthy-Welch Exchange"; emphasis added).

when he said that virtues can and do disappear when they are not practiced regularly. *Basic decency must be normative, and behavior to the contrary must be considered peripheral and inappropriate.*

The values described here give individuals a personal plumb line for self-judgment and self-correction; they also give us common ground for holding accountable the people who violate these basic normative rules. I know that involves "judgment," but we are judging normative behavior, not personal worth. After all, we exercise our judgment all the time based on a variety of ideas of good and bad behavior. The CORTHODOX Way gives us a common value system that can supplement and reinforce the norms we need to protect. We are always monitoring the behavior of other people, using tradition, upbringing, geographic influences, political party positions, generational norms, religious affiliation, and media choices. We are always judging both ourselves and others. This set of core values can give us common ground as we discern whom and what we will support with our efforts, our time, and our money.

People without core values are too often victims of influential/manipulative individuals, destructive movements, cons, and ideologies. I hope you find the CORTHODOX values described here to be empowering guideposts. Do not drift through life by the seat of your pants! Do not be the victim of propaganda, phony people, or manipulative media. Stay away from that briar patch!

I sound like a Pilates instructor when I tell you: "You need a strong core!" Without core values, you will not be strong enough to stand tall in this world. It is in your best interest to build a clear, positive personal identity on principles that provide an infrastructure for your actions. The CORTHODOX Way will help you do that.

In summary, what follows is a description of nine values for both secular and religious people, values that are most likely to have good outcomes for you personally and for society. CORTHODOX decency values can serve you as a practical tool for becoming a better person and for discerning the sort of people you want to befriend, marry, vote for, and work with. These values will give you a center, a way of judging, thinking, and being in the world, and a community of like-minded people.[18] Once internalized, you will *know* what *you* do in various situations before those situations arise. Maybe you will teach your children the CORTHODOX values? Maybe

18. *Ortho* is a Greek word meaning "straight" or "orthodox," like an orthodontist gives you straight teeth. CORTHODOX gives you a set of core values.

these values will be found useful to corporations, institutions of all types, including educational and international ones? Dear reader, that will be up to you.

This treatise is me "doing" something; it is my offering, an example of a person acting and sharing to make a difference. Hopeful people look at the world straight on, imagine what might be different, then work to make it so. Rebecca Solnit says: "Hope is not like a lottery ticket you can sit on the sofa and clutch, feeling lucky. Hope is an axe you break down doors with."[19] Let's be brave and do just that. After all, we are all in this together.

RELEVANT QUOTES AND TOPICS TO PONDER

"As the world gets more deeply intertwined, everyone's behavior—the values that each of us bring to this interdependent world—matters more than ever. . . . So does the 'Golden Rule.' . . . Because more people in more places in more ways on more days can now do unto you and you unto them like never before."
—Thomas L. Friedman, *How We Broke the World*

"It's not about what we say or think, but what we do that defines us."
—Andrew Davies, *Jane Austen's "Sense & Sensibility"*

"Character is destiny."
—William Falk, *Week*, Mar. 26, 2021

"The whole house of the womb of nature is properly and completely lighted by the lamp of history which destroys the darkness of ignorance."
—Adi Parva, the first of eighteen books that make up the *Mahabharata*, an epic poem of ancient India

"There are many things we can live without. Self-respect is not one of them."
—Vivian Gomick, *Week*, Oct. 8, 2021

"What you believe in your head asks almost nothing of you. Lifestyle asks everything of us, and every day, and on ever new levels of choice.

19. Rebecca Solnit, as quoted in *Week*, "Wit and Wisdom."

It is a journey that never stops . . . never totally succeeds; you are never totally right."
—Richard Rohr, Center for Action and Contemplation, Jan. 6, 2010

"A faultless man I cannot hope ever to meet; the most I can hope for is to meet a man of fixed principles."
—Confucius, "The Analects"

Compassionate (C)

Empathetic, Charitable, Kind, Community Minded

We experience compassion and empathy in part through our imagination. I can imagine that what is happening to you will, or could, happen to me. If we have had similar experiences ourselves, we remember how we felt, and we recognize the emotions and challenges of people in analogous situations. At these times, the "selfhood" that dominates our lives relaxes enough that we allow a sort of connective tissue of empathy to form between us and someone else. Empathy is expressed by acts of compassion. Caring people offer help. People at least listen, without shoehorning in to tell their own similar story (an interruption difficult to resist because it indicates common ground, but save it for later.)

Over time most people develop the ability to sense or imagine what it feels like to be someone else in a particular situation. Sharing stories with others helps us cope, gives us a source of ideas and information, and builds friendship bonds, assuming we are wise enough to share with trustworthy people. We trust people who listen nonjudgmentally and with openhearted compassion. Sometimes it is you who needs to talk; sometimes it is me. We connect. We share. We support. We perform acts of kindness.

Humans thrive best in a community of this sort. Conflictual communities create anxiety, distrust, and internal questions. Dis-ease develops, then outright fear. Soon people are wondering: "Should I leave this place?" or "Do I need a gun?!" In cities people often avoid eye contact. Gadgets abound, and people everywhere are "plugged in" and often absent from other people. Where money keeps everything in motion and bestows status, safety, and identity, compassion is not only undervalued, but it may also be seen as a weakness.

Wang Yang-Ming (1472–1529 CE) served in the imperial civil service of Ming China during a period of imperial decline (ca. 1450–1550.) In his work *The Inquiry on the Great Learning*, he focused less attention on self-realization and the study of the external world and more attention on moral revitalization. He believed that "great men" regard heaven and earth and the myriad occupants thereof as one body.[1]

For Wang Yang-Ming, empathy and compassion are a natural consequence of the realization that we are part of a larger whole. He argued that humaneness exists in the "small" man *and* the "great" man. Almost everyone who sees a child about to fall into a well will feel alarm and take action to prevent the injury. When the frightened cries of animals about to be slaughtered are heard, a sense of pity is felt. This is the "humanity" (humaneness) of a mind that has not been aroused and corrupted by selfishness, greed, or fear of harm. When one's mind is obscured by self-centered desires, it becomes smaller, divided, and easily stirred by anger. In some cases, one may even slaughter one's own brothers.[2] Wang Yang-Ming writes as follows:

> Everything from ruler, minister, husband, wife and friends to mountains, rivers, spiritual beings, birds, animals, and plants should be truly loved in order to realize my humanity that forms one body. . . .
>
> The nature endowed in us by heaven is pure and perfect. . . . It is the original substance of the *clear character* which is called innate knowledge of the good. As the highest good emanates and reveals itself, we will consider right as right and wrong as wrong. . . . There can be no consideration of adding to or subtracting from it. . . .
>
> Manifesting the clear character and loving the people are in essence one and the same, this is the default mode of the tranquil, original mind that is not perturbed by error.[3]

1. In 1950, in a letter to a grieving friend, Albert Einstein took a similar position. "A human being is a part of the whole, . . . a part limited in time and space. He experiences himself, his thoughts, and feelings as something separate from the rest—a kind of optical delusion . . . of his consciousness. The striving to free oneself from this delusion is the one issue of true religion. Not to nourish it but to try to overcome it is the way to reach . . . peace of mind. . . . Our task must be to free ourselves from this prison by widening our circle of compassion to embrace all living creatures and the whole of nature in its beauty" (Duda, "One with Everything?").

2. Yang-Ming, "Inquiry on Great Learning," 301–2.

3. Yang-Ming, "Inquiry on Great Learning," 304–5; emphasis added.

Questions abound in both psychology and philosophy regarding "having" and "developing" compassion. Are we born with the gift of a clear mind and clear character as Wang Yang-Ming argues? Are we born with a blank-slate mind with no a priori knowledge, as John Locke (d. 1704) asserted? Are we born flawed and in need of being rescued from our human flaws and transformed by the grace of God as St. Augustine (d. 430 CE) says we are? Perhaps you agree with Immanuel Kant (d. 1804), who says we come into the world with a conscience and reason and can recognize and determine "moral imperatives" that are necessary for right order and basic virtue.

People tend to develop a default point of view about compassion based on their own experiences. Are you generally a negative thinker when it comes to humans' capacity for virtue and goodness (a.k.a. a low view of humanity)? Or do you typically expect humans to be more kind than cruel, more good than bad, and more compassionate than vengeful (a.k.a. a high view of humanity)? You are probably thinking to yourself, "It depends on the day." Indeed, it does. And, it depends on how other people have treated you.

Are all human beings capable of living compassionately?[4] Can compassion be learned? How does compassion form in people? Certainly, priorities shift with life phases. As one ages, the details of life, such as how you made a living, how important you were in the company or institution in which you worked, your savings/investment account, and whether you finished your "bucket list" fades.

What becomes important near the end of life is relationships, particularly familial relationships. People self-examine and wonder if the impact they have had on the world was generally good. They assess their contribution. I have been to my share of funerals and heard enough eulogies about the deceased to recognize this: the primary measure of a person's character is ultimately in their capacity for compassion, kindness, charitable action, and empathetic camaraderie with various people. What follows here is a letter to the editor that makes this point beautifully:

4. See Center for Contemplative Science and Compassion-Based Ethics, "Overview of CBCT." This program at Emory is designed to help people develop more compassion. The assumption is that compassion is a skill that can be developed and expanded. Doing so benefits both giver and receiver. Beyond the individual, compassion contributes to a kinder and more just world.

> My father died when he was 84, and when he was 80 years old, I asked if he'd had any regrets in his life. "I wish I'd been more kind," he said. For me those words were revelatory. I am an impatient person (as was my dad), and as I try to improve myself as I move forward in life, the idea and practice of kindness have become my personal motivating force. Everything improves with kindness, and I've come to learn that it goes a long way in helping me to overcome my natural inclinations to rush, to brush off, to dismiss out of some misguided notion of my own importance. This has been a tough year for all of us, and when I'm in a fix, or confused about how to proceed in some thorny situation, or even when given an opportunity to interact with my fellow humans, my father's words come to me. I hope I will not have a similar regret if I'm ever asked that question at the end of my life.[5]

Can compassion be enhanced or acquired by training? Psychologists identify three orientations of compassion: 1) compassion for others, 2) receiving compassion from others, and 3) self-compassion. According to Kristin Neff, PhD, self-compassion is defined as "being open to and moved by one's own suffering, experiencing feelings of caring and kindness toward oneself, taking an understanding, nonjudgmental attitude toward one's inadequacies and failures, and recognizing that one's own experience is part of the common human experience."[6] People who are "hard on themselves" or have overly high self-expectations often suffer from depression and anxiety, i.e., the fear of messing up.

A Stanford team of experts conducted a study with one hundred adults over nine weeks to determine if compassion can be taught and how. They identified four key components of compassion: 1) an awareness of suffering (cognitive/empathic awareness), 2) sympathetic concern or being emotionally moved by suffering (affective component), 3) a wish to see the relief of that suffering (intention), and 4) a responsiveness or readiness to help relieve that suffering (motivational).[7]

Participants in the study acknowledged improvements in awareness of suffering leading to compassion for others, receiving compassion from others, and self-compassion. The results of the study indicate that compassion can be intentionally cultivated in a training program that involves

5. McSorley, "Codes That Guide," para. 1.

6. Neff's numerous works on mindful self-compassion are listed in the sources list of an article by Jazaieri et al., "Enhancing Compassion."

7. Jazaieri et al., "Enhancing Compassion."

meditation practices. Simply put, compassion is not simply an intuitive "gift."

Compassionate mind training is useful for people with elevated levels of shame, depression, and a tendency to feel inferior. Kristin Neff, PhD, and colleagues are currently developing a program called Mindful Self-Compassion, which focuses on cultivating self-compassion.[8]

While individuals vary in their baseline empathic capacities, a person's capacity for empathy and concern can be somewhat modulated with training. Self-empathy is a good first step.[9]

The ability to discern the feelings of others is like "smartness" or "creativity"; we have it in degrees. Just as some of us are smarter or more creative than others, some of us are more empathetic than others. What if you lack empathy or have it in small measure? People who feel less empathy are typically quite me-centered. Some of them are narcissists.

Narcissists want to control the situation and decide what is to be decided. They manipulate others by bullying, crying to show hurt or disappointment, demanding, and/or criticizing. Their prey are empaths who want to please others and "get along" without confrontation. Eventually the empath feels powerless, depressed, and/or angry enough to exit the relationship, or worse, he or she does not exit the relationship and loses personal autonomy. Narcissists are nearly always thinking and talking about what they "want." They use people to move toward a desired end. They do not "feel" wrong or bad because they do not empathize with the other person. They will stay connected to those who serve their wants and needs as long as possible. When their "servant(s)" no longer want to continue the relationship, the narcissist will cry out, condemn, or punish the person who disappoints. If they can no longer get their way, they will separate from their victim and move on. Children and spouses of narcissists typically need supportive counseling to reclaim their autonomy.

Taken a step further than the self-centeredness of the manipulative narcissist is the psychopath. Psychopaths are cold and remorseless, incapable of empathy, manipulative, self-focused, impulsive, and typically bound by their inner nature to harm or act with violence towards others. Robert Hare made efforts to identify psychopaths. He studied prisoners. Hare determined that psychopaths were "emotionally deaf." They simply do not have the capacity to feel what more sympathetic people feel. Emotions

8. Jazaieri et al., "Enhancing Compassion."

9. Van Marrewijk, "3 Elements of Self-Compassion."

like empathy, remorse, and love cannot be aroused in them. A photo of a chair and a photo of a ghastly death do not cause different reactions in the mind of the psychopath. Neurons do not fire. Psychopaths have the same "blank-slate" reaction to both photographs.[10]

According to Hare, explaining empathetic caring to a psychopath is like trying to explain the color "red" to a color-blind person. People must experience red to know what it is. "Red" cannot be taught; it must be experienced. For scientific and professional acceptance Hare needed a way to identify psychopathic behaviors, measure them, and assess people. He and Steven Hart, his former student and a respected expert in this field, created a test for psychopathy. They concluded that the traits of psychopaths are these: egocentricity, a grandiose sense of self-worth, pathological lying, cunning, manipulative behavior, lack of sincerity, lack of remorse or guilt, and *lack of empathy.* Psychopaths are also sensation seeking and prone to boredom, and typically fail to accept responsibility for their own actions.[11]

For our purposes, the point in mentioning the traits of narcissists and psychopaths is to recognize variation in human beings. People fall somewhere on a spectrum for empathy and compassion.[12] Some people lack it; some people have lots of it. Consider the Albanian nun who devoted herself to giving dying people in India a dignified death. Mother Theresa (d. 1997) was canonized for her service to the poorest of the poor and is on one end of the spectrum; a psychopath is on the other end. To have empathy is to know that we are tied together in our humanity. Empaths recognize and celebrate the successes and joys of another person, and they listen and act compassionately.

Through empathy we can understand the oneness of creation and the wrongness of seeing people as "other" than ourselves. By listening empathetically, we are attentive enough to be understanding, helpful, and observant. Compassion is acting on that empathy. Once we *understand* the troubles or suffering of another person, we can *act* compassionately and take some action to help. Sometimes all that is needed is to listen with an

10. Are you superficially charming? Do you have a grandiose sense of self-worth? Are you manipulative in getting what you want? Controlling and need to be in charge? Do you lack remorse for the consequences of your behavior?

11. *Encyclopedia of Mental Disorders*, "Hare Psychopathy Checklist."

12. See Howard, *Stop Manipulating Me!*, 14–17. Scans of people with this disorder have less gray matter in the cerebral cortex of the brain structure in the area that regulates emotion and cognitive functioning.

open heart. Sometimes we share resources we have that the other person needs, or we offer guidance to decrease discomfort.

In an interview with Sister Dorothy Stoner, Taha Najem, a workforce readiness specialist for the St. Benedict Education Center, explains that he was once a translator for the US military in Iraq. He says: "When someone comes to me, if I can help, I will do it. It's how my mother and father raised me, and my schooling. . . . Look at your fingers, they are not the same; all are different, like people, but they are one hand!"[13]

Taha Najem recognizes the connectedness of everyone to everyone else, to creation itself, and to the Creator. Sometimes I need a hand, sometimes you need a hand. We are connected as a human family in that we all have needs, and we rely on the empathy, compassion, and actions of other people.

In one of his meditations on empathy and connectivity, Richard Rohr wrote the following:

> There are no *higher* and *lower* in this world. There is no *smart*; no *stupid*; no *totally right or totally wrong*. The only meaningful division is between those who *serve* and those who allow themselves to be *served*. All the rest is temporary posturing. . . . We must learn to stand in two different places and to change places often. The served must also be the servants, and the servants must also be the served.[14]

Kindness, empathy, and compassion are modern terms that connect to the more traditional concept of "charity." Faith, hope, and charity (love) are the Christian virtues. They were added to the four classical virtues described by Plato: temperance, justice, prudence, and fortitude. "Charity" is more complex than you might think. The word "charity" has Latin roots; it is derived from the Latin word *caritas*, meaning "one who cares," one who cares for the poor and needy with time and personal resources, one who takes action to benefit people other than themselves.

Charity can be expressed as emotional, spiritual, or material comfort. It is a way of being in the world. What is this connectivity to other humans that leads to humaneness, even self-sacrifice? Charity goes beyond keeping commandments. It is mercy, sympathy, empathy, compassion, and love.

13. Romey, "Brothers and Sisters," 11.

14. Richard Rohr is a Franciscan friar and the founder of the Center for Action and Contemplation. Full text had been found at https://stpaulsbremerton.org/wp-content/uploads/2020/10/From-the-Halls-of-St.-Pauls-10-29-20.pdf. Link discontinued.

In Latin translations of the Greek New Testament, "charity" is the translation of the Greek word *agape* (love). In First Corinthians, the well-known treatise on love, Paul writes that "love is patient and kind; not jealous or boastful." At the end of the chapter, he writes: "So faith, hope and love abide . . . but the greatest of these is love" (1 Cor 13:13).

Jesus was able to look past specific behaviors out of love for the person. He tells his followers *to love* the least among us, even our enemies and our persecutors. Imagine how Peter felt after he had denied Jesus three times! Three times Jesus told him to forget about it. I'm over it. If you want to make it up to me: "Feed my sheep," i.e., practice compassion. When Jesus is suffering and dying on the cross, he prays with compassion for his persecutors in an almost unbelievable prayer: "Forgive them, for they know not what they do" (Luke 23:34).[15]

Jesus does not call his followers to "act right" or else. (He breaks rules sometimes too.) He calls them to love the least among them, to love their enemies, i.e., to love as he loves. Love is a fundamental message of the Gospels. When Christians engage in philanthropic charity, they are not so much acting out of pity or duty or obedience to a law. They are acting out of love and compassion.

In more rules-centered traditions, charity is thought of partly as a discipline. In Judaism, charitable acts are associated with "justice," particularly social justice. The "grumpy" prophet Amos writes:[16] "They have sold the poor person for a pair of sandals; they trample on the head of the poor and push them out of their way" (Amos 8:6). For Jews, acts of philanthropy are *tzedakah* and *mitzvah*—that which is right, just, and commanded, and perhaps also a kind act of goodwill. In Judaism one who gives *tzedakah* is acting justly; one who does not give is acting unjustly or mean-spiritedly.[17] In other words, people who ignore the poor disobey God.

One of the Five Pillars of Islam is zakah or zakat or a donation of 2.5 percent. (This donation is calculated differently in varying Muslim traditions.) The zakah donation is the minimum amount one is expected to give. Wealthy Muslims often regard their wealth as a loan from Allah, so practicing charity may be a duty, but it is also an expression of gratitude,

15. See also Biblical Hermeneutics, "What Did Jesus Mean."

16. My father had Amos as his middle name, so I read this Old Testament book several times. I kept wondering what my grandmother had been thinking!

17. For a more thorough discussion of the charitable expectations for Jews, see Telushkin, "Charity."

and gratitude prevents greed; gratitude is considered a high virtue. Also, generosity is thought to be rewarded in the afterlife. Muslims use the word *sadaqah* to refer to a spectrum of various voluntary acts of kindness and compassion.

The practice of cultivating generosity by means of charitable acts and alms is also in the Indian Vedic tradition. In chapter 87 of Hinduism's Vedic work the Adi Parva, sweet speech and the kind refusal to use harsh words or to wrong others, *even those who have wronged you*, is regarded as a form of charity. This "charity of the spirit" requires no monetary gift at all. In the Adi Parva of the Hindu epic *Mahabharata*, chapter 91, people are encouraged to acquire wealth by honest means and to use their wealth to practice charity and hospitality toward others.[18]

In Buddhism, four widely revered bodhisattvas (meaning Buddhas to be) are held in high regard throughout Asia: 1) Kannon Bosatsu (boundless compassion), 2) Monju Bosatsu (a.k.a. Manjushri) (wisdom), 3) Fugen Bosatsu (practice, because living ethically frees the mind from angst), and 4) Jizo Bosatsu (vast patience). Bodhisattvas achieved Buddhahood (enlightenment) and could have exited the life cycle, but they chose to remain in the world rather than entering nirvana. Doing so is a great act of compassion and empathy for people who suffer. Buddhists admire leaders who express "loving-kindness" or warm-hearted concern for the well-being of other people. His Holiness the Dalai Lama has declared, "My religion is kindness."[19]

In summary, compassion is expressed by acts and attitude, by kindness, love, gratitude, duty, and/or personal generosity. Throughout the centuries, decent individuals have learned the value and rewards of compassionate practices. We *are* like fingers on a hand. We need each other. All religious traditions offer their adherents a call, a challenge, even a command to help the vulnerable, poor, stranger, orphan, the troubled, and the weak or infirm.

The US has various kinds of people scattered across a multitude of communities. Here, pluralism is typical, not rare. Our ability to pull together rather than living with a "me-first" mindset that splits us into warring camps is a major theme in our country's success story. The families who settled on the prairie helped each other survive in a harsh place. People of

18. For a beginner's introduction to Hinduism and Buddhism, see Gettysburg College, "What Is Hinduism?"

19. Snelling, *Buddhist Handbook*, 84.

all sorts were part of military units that fought against Fascism in World War II. We are at our best when we pull together, no matter the race or creed. Doing so is taking part in a grand story of both unity and pluralism.

What does compassion look like in the modern era when more people (83 percent) live in cities? In a global context, who are our "neighbors"? Community-minded efforts must be invented to meet new needs. Instead of barn raising, we could help with Habitat for Humanity housing, for example, or we could work to increase access to healthy food, education, and health care.

- What if we tempered our rugged individualism to develop a community spirit? What would that look like?
- What if all capable people participated in at least one way to make their community more unified, more coherent, more supportive, kinder, and more humane?
- Why do you think the applications of college students emphasize participation in community projects? Can you name similar expectations for other groups?

Cities and communities evolved around shared values, goals, and ideals, including profit, religious heritage, tribal identity, historical stories, and shared struggles that link people to each other by way of common experiences and challenges. CORTHODOX decency values can play a unifying influence, especially if these values are taught to young people in religious and/or educational institutions and in youth organizations. Interestingly, some cities have become "compassionate cities."[20]

The Athenian philosopher Plato (ca. 427–348 BCE), was not that concerned with a state that promotes the material well-being of citizen inhabitants. He wanted people to prepare for and live a "good" life, and he expected cultural and political leaders to play a role in helping them do so. For him, life divided into a public and private sphere was a source of unhappy division that could not be good for individuals or the state. He considered good people, good government, and the good state to be essential to the good

20. Austin, TX and Asheville, NC, along with other cities have embraced the goal of becoming a compassionate city. For more on this movement, see https://charterforcompassion.org/austin-texas; https://charterforcompassion.org/what-makes-a-compassionate-city-cci; https://excellencereporter.com/exclusive-interviews-on-the-meaning-of-life/what-makes-a-compassionate-city/.

life and to the promotion of virtue.[21] In Plato's ideal world, there would be no "fake news," because misleading people and lying would not be normal behavior, and wealth and class would be less important than living virtuously in an interconnected society.

Plato's pragmatic student, Aristotle (384–322 BCE), argued that "poverty is the parent of revolution and crime."[22] He argued that strong communities have a strong middle class, and that government, businesses, and community-minded people should take action to support and build a large middle class, because a community of haves and have-nots is unstable. In short, everyone in a community benefits from the stability that results from less economic division.

Greek communities were small city-states. We live in nation-states connected to other nation-states by transportation, various and speedy forms of communication, and shared interests. Our world is smaller and more connected than ever. Climate change, like the world wars of the twentieth century, reminds us of our connections.

After the destruction of World War II, hopeful people set out to rebuild a better world and to promote peace. The United Nations was created, as were world courts and the World Health Organization. The Universal Declaration of Human Rights was written.[23] We can easily see the divergence from the goals laid out for the postwar world in our own era. Yet, nothing else has replaced the hope-filled efforts of that era.

In our time ambitious leaders try to take territory, control communications, and use the internet to influence people in countries other than their own. Aggressive, expansionist forms of nationalism have reemerged, and efforts to live into the post–World War II vision have floundered. Are the goals set in the late 1940s still valuable enough to pursue? Do they inspire us still? Have we given up on a peaceful, interconnected world because the lessons of World War II have faded or for other reasons? Is it time to review, reassess, and revise the Universal Declaration of Human Rights?

We need compassionate people of all sorts to work together on common goals and multiple fronts. Our problems and issues are numerous (climate change, stark economic inequality fed by personal greed, violence, addiction, pandemics, mental health, and access to expertise), but we too are many. We need cordial international relationships, because what we do

21. Tomlin, *Great Philosophers*, 46.

22. https://www.goodreads.com/author/quotes/2192.Aristotle.

23. United Nations, "Universal Declaration."

and what "they" do matters. It is easier to work with and alongside all kinds of people when you we share the CORTHODOX values. Power, wealth, and one-upmanship can be set aside to focus on more noble goals. More than ever, we humans are all in this together. This is not the era to be all about "me and mine." Instead, what you *do* affects me too.

CORTHODOX people—that is, compassionate, disciplined, humble, responsible, trustworthy, open-minded, xenial people—would ideally be at the helm at every level of government and society. They would also be the typical or normative people who serve as leaders who give more than they take. While we may not enjoy or like everyone who crosses our paths, we can refuse to reject them, ignore them, or cause them harm. We must also be honest, respectful, and brave enough to question and challenge self-centeredness, greed, and disrespect toward other people. That means indecent people who lack decency values must confront not unkindness but some degree of social estrangement.

One example of this is when Joseph Welch called out the populist Senator Joseph McCarthy in 1954, asking him, "Have you no sense of decency, sir?"[24] We can be kind, present to people, and simultaneously supportive of basic decency values. To live in a world of "anything goes" is to live in a chaotic, damaging, diverse world of self-centered individualism. It is a world that isolates this group from that group, these people from those people. It divides and undermines humane kindness toward others.

The Catholic vision of the common good is described in the "Compendium of the Social Doctrine of the Church." Human rights, as described in the compendium, include access to food, housing, work, education, culture, transportation, basic health care, freedom of communication and expression, and the protection of religious freedom. The Catholic Church's social doctrine is meant to guide both simple and powerful people to build a more compassionate society.

24. Joseph Nye Welch (Oct. 22, 1890—Oct. 6, 1960) was an American lawyer who served as the chief counsel for the US Army while it was under investigation for Communist activities by Senator Joseph McCarthy's Senate Permanent Subcommittee on Investigations, a.k.a. the Army-McCarthy hearings. His confrontation with McCarthy during the hearings, in which he asked McCarthy "Have you no sense of *decency*, sir, at long last?," is seen as a turning point in the history of McCarthyism (emphasis added). (McCarthy was on a witch hunt for Communists in the State Department because he wanted to boost his political profile.) The moment was a turning point at a time when television was new and impactful. These websites are both interesting and telling: Democracy Now!, "Where's My Roy Cohn?"; and History.com Editors, "Have You No Sense." Note the role played by Roy Cohn.

Another "social doctrine," more secular in nature but like the social doctrine of the Catholic Church, is the UN Universal Declaration of Human Rights. The human rights articles, which concern states, require a commitment to peace, a sound judicial system, protection of the environment, and the provision of essential services to all.[25]

At the end of World War II in September 1945, people looked around at the horrible destruction, misery, deaths, and displacements and committed themselves to building up democratic institutions and righting the wrongs of the past by imagining a different future. The systematic execution of Jews by the Nazi regime in Germany horrified people around the world. Following the racist and far-right nationalistic policies of fascism adopted by Italy and Nazi Germany, a basic statement of human rights was needed. The context of the post–World War II era provoked a willingness to try.[26]

If a free press exists, exposure of human rights violations cannot be hidden from the world. Obstacles are many, but information can be only somewhat contained. A formal list of human rights was written after the Holocaust and the other horrors of World War II. Fifty-six countries signed on to create world cooperation around a set of common human values. The hope was that governments would no longer attempt to exterminate minorities and specific groups inside their borders, nor would they try to expand their borders beyond the ones set at the end of World War II. Power would not justify claims to seized territory. Intimidation would be subdued by international communities, established borders, and mutual respect.[27]

The practice of human decency is never *only* about individual ethical development. Our virtues and vices are writ large in our public values, and our public values are at least partially reflected in our laws and in the elected leaders we choose. How could it be otherwise? In Western democracies, the state *is* us. State leaders "serve" us when they hold office.

---

25. On Dec. 10, 1948, fifty-six countries, including China, gathered at the United Nations headquarters in Paris to sign the Universal Declaration of Human Rights. Eight member states decided to abstain: the USSR, Ukraine, Belorussia, Czechoslovakia, Poland, Yugoslavia, Saudi Arabia, and South Africa. (Ukraine and Belorussia, although union republics of the USSR, had been granted separate status as member states of the United Nations, as requested by Stalin.) (Patenaude, "Perspectives on Human Rights").

26. Official casualty sources estimate military deaths at nearly fifteen to twenty-one million and civilian deaths at thirty-eight to fifty million (Defense Casualty Analysis System, "World War II"; National WWII Museum, "Research Starters").

27. The Rohingya people of Myanmar, who were forced to flee the country of Myanmar, suffered genocide and expulsion in 2017 and are considered one of the most persecuted minorities in the world.

"The West," says David Brooks, "is not an ethnic designation or an elitist country club. . . . It is a moral accomplishment, and unlike its rivals, it aspires to extend dignity, human rights, and self-determination to all. . . . That's worth reforming and working on and defending and sharing in the decades ahead."[28]

Compassionate people develop "sympathetic joy" (*mudita*), a caring humaneness that is the opposite of the hard-hearted competitiveness in which we engage to "prove" ourselves as wiser, more "together," or superior, morally or economically.

RELEVANT QUOTES AND TOPICS TO PONDER

- Sometimes business leaders collaborate with people and organizations of goodwill to be community partners and to enhance their community's well-being. Recently top earners, i.e., billionaires, have received exorbitant pay and live an indulgent life. They are national heroes in some ways, certainly important influencers. Can you name billionaires (or successful people) who have profited greatly and used that profit for the benefit of individuals and/or for the general welfare out of a sense of giving back or doing good?
- Why do we give? Is it right to expect the very rich to do the giving because it would be less burdensome for them, or is it important for all of us to give beyond ourselves and our families? Why?
- It is unwise to think that religious tolerance means "everything goes" when it comes to religion. Separation of church and state is assumed in a free society. Even so, Christian nationalists often disagree with this principle. What characterizes this form of spiritualism? What are their perceived threats? What are their goals?[29]
- Fifty years ago, the conservative economist Milton Freeman told American executives: "There is one and only one social responsibility of business—to use its resources and engage in activities designed to increase its profits so long as it stays within the rules of the game."[30]

28. D. Brooks, "Culture Wars," final para.

29. See O'Brien, "Christian Nationalism"; Christian Nationalism Research; Maiden, "New Apostolic Reformation."

30. Zuboff, "You Are the Object," para. 32.

Question: What *are* the "rules of the game"? Who makes the rules? Who and what influences the rule makers? Competitive businesses sometimes put profit over people and country. What role does government play in reducing the damage this causes?

- The Supreme Court has ruled that businesses are "people" (kind of). They pay taxes and can give donations to election campaigns. The result of this ruling is an influx of money to political leaders now dependent on it, and a weakening of the voice of the people who vote and make no or smaller contributions.

  If businesses are people, what else might we expect from them other than taxes? What forms of compassion might we hope for from the medical and pharmaceutical industry? Gun dealers? Industries that cause harm to the environment?

- Ryan Bussey, author *of Gunfight: My Battle Against the Industry That Radicalized America*, tells a good story. He worked for a gun manufacturing company for twenty years and grew up with guns, as did most people who came of age on ranches in the Western US. But Bussey turned on the National Rifle Association and his industry *for purposely keeping people upset, in a perpetual simmer of fear and anger.* Bussey noticed the real goal of scaring people: gun sales. Fearful, outraged people buy more guns.

  Many people care deeply about the consequences of easy access to weaponry, as well as the constitutional right to bear arms. Where do the outrage and the compassion belong? For the dead and wounded? With gun owners and their rights? With the right of businesses to profit?

- In her book *The Age of Surveillance Capitalism*, Dr. Shoshana Zuboff describes how our minds, and posts, have been mined for data and how technology has damaged and undermined social society and democracy. How have misinformation and manipulation weakened the populace's unity and common purpose.

"We do not have to live in the world the new technocrats are designing for us. . . . No more algorithmic feedbags. No more infrastructure to make the people less powerful and the powerful more controlling. Every day we vote with our attention; it is precious, and desperately

wanted by those who will use it against us for their own profit and political goals. Don't let them."
—Adrienne LaFrance, *Atlantic*, Mar. 2024

"This kindness, this stupid kindness, is what is most truly human in a human being."
—Vasily Grossman, *Week*, May 12, 2023

"Too often we underestimate the power of a touch, a smile, a kind word, a listening ear, an honest compliment, or the smallest act of caring, all of which have the potential to turn a life around."
—Attributed to Leo Buscaglia

"Let us temper our criticism with kindness. None of us comes fully equipped."
—Carl Sagan, *The Demon-Haunted World* (The work from which this sentence is extracted is worthy of reading/discussing.)

The major religions have sayings like the Christian Golden Rule. Here are some of them. These concise sayings advise compassion and empathy for others:

"Therefore, whatever you desire for people to do to you, so also you should do to them; for this is the Law and the Prophets." (Matt 7:12)

"Not one of you truly believes until you wish for others what you wish for yourself."
—Muhammad, Hadith 13, 40 Hadith an-Nawawi

"This is the sum of duty: do not do to others what would cause pain if done to you."
—Hinduism, *Mahabharata* 5:1517

"Treat no others in ways that you yourself would find hurtful."
—The Buddha, Udana-Varga 5.18

"What you do not want done to yourself, do not do to others."
—Confucius, "The Analects"

> "And it is so simple . . . The one thing is—love thy neighbor as thyself—that is the one thing. That is all, nothing else is needed. You will instantly find how to live."
> —Fyodor Dostoyevsky, *The Dream of a Ridiculous Man*

> "It's just not something that is natural. You have to be taught the way of peace, the way of love, the way of nonviolence. And in the religious sense, in the moral sense, you can say in the bosom of every human being, there is a spark of the divine. So, you don't have a right as a human to abuse that spark of the divine in your fellow human beings."
> —John Lewis, interview with Krista Tippett, *On Being*

> "All human lives are too various and alive with contradiction to be neatly classed into the categories in which we try to contain the chaos of life, and yet we spend so much of our own unclassifiable lives classing the lives of others. One measure of kindness might be the unwillingness to crush complexity into category, the refusal to lash others with our labels."
> —Maria Popova, *Marginalian*

> "The sins of the flesh are not the gravest sins. The gravest ones are more 'angelic.'"
> —Pope Francis I (He goes on to mention hate and pride.)

Episcopal Bishop Michael Curry placed an emphasis on our responsibility to the common good. We are to work for a good, just, humane, and loving society by standing up for what is right and sometimes marching in the streets. It means praying and participating in society and "fashioning a civic order that reflects goodness, justice, and compassion."

> "In the United States and in the world, we have different cultures, different politics, different experiences that have shaped our beliefs. But if we can establish that we are working toward some common good, whether we like each other or not, then we can be brothers and sisters. Let's all stop worrying about whether we like each other and choose to believe instead that we're capable of doing good together."
> —Michael Curry with Sara Grace, *Love Is the Way: Holding on to Hope in Troubling Times*

"In its truest sense, religion should reconnect human beings—bind them again—to the creation, to one another, to the Divine, to Love. Rituals, song, prayer, preaching, reflection, dancing, meditation—all of these religious practices are intended to bind us together in love and restrain us from harming one another. Religion should reconnect us to the ground of our being, to the source of our existence. . . . Religion should help us see how our biases about color, gender, sexuality, and class cause deep hurt to both body and soul.

Unfortunately, religion is too often weaponized. Wars are waged in the name of religion. People are enslaved and terrorized in the name of religion. Wealth has been amassed on the backs of the poor in the name of religion. . . . Jews were exterminated, in the name of a poor, brown, *Jewish* baby who was at one time homeless and at another a refugee.

If humankind is to thrive, we need to let go of any religion that wounds and kills. Some of what we believe about God is actually *about us*; at times we create God in our own image. . . . Some of us imagine *God* as punitive, angry, and vengeful because these are aspects of ourselves that make us feel powerful and protected, rather than vulnerable. But we need to exercise a spiritual imagination free of fear and shed the constraints of unhealthy religion. Hate-filled religion needs an exorcism."
—Jacqui Lewis, *Fierce Love: A Bold Path to Ferocious Courage and Rule-Breaking Kindness That Can Heal the World*

"Of the many radical things said and done by Jesus, his unflinching emphasis on *love* was most radical of all. Love was the greatest commandment, . . . his prime directive—love for God, for self, for neighbor, for stranger, for alien, for outsider, for outcast, and even for enemy, as he himself modeled. The new commandment of love [John 13:34] meant that neither beliefs nor words, neither taboos, systems, structures nor the labels that enshrined them mattered most. Love decentered everything else; love relativized everything else; love took priority over everything else—everything."
–Brian McLaren, Center for Action and Contemplation, Feb. 21, 2023

"Love is ultimately measured by people's capacity to see and care about the other person *as they are*; succeeding in this effort is how people in relationships grow."
—Orna Guralnik, *New York Times Magazine*, June 21, 2023

"A great deal of our onslaught on Mother Nature is not really lack of intelligence but a lack of compassion for future generations and the health of the planet: sheer selfish greed for short-term benefits to increase the wealth and power of individuals, corporations, and governments. The rest is due to thoughtlessness, lack of education and poverty. In other words, there seems to be a disconnect between our clever brain and our compassionate heart. True wisdom requires both thinking with our head and understanding with our heart."
—Jane Goodall, *The Book of Hope: A Survival Guide for Trying Times*

"Imagine that you have just died . . . and you enter heaven. . . . The presence of God seems to pervade everyone and everything. . . . People are humble and genuinely interested in others. . . . It is a place of true freedom, trust, and intimacy. . . . People of all cultures and languages and times retain . . . their uniqueness. . . . No one argues, no one fights, no one hates, and no one complains . . . because they accept and love one another completely. They are fully alive. . . . Now I want you to imagine that someone has walked beside you through that doorway of death. . . . That person has lived his life cramped in hatred and fear, tight in guilt and greed, ingrown in lust and selfishness. He has spent every day of his life complaining and being bitter and blaming others and being ungrateful. He has been suspicious of those different from himself, and he has become an expert at lying and cheating and using others. He is proud, arrogant, unwilling to admit he is wrong. . . . Could the acceptance and love and trust and openness that welcome you seem to him disgusting, weak, terrifying, insipid, or repulsive? . . . Sometimes I wonder if hell is just what heaven feels like for those who haven't learned in this life what this life is intended to teach. . . . I believe with all my heart that God is not willing for even one person to miss out on the joy and glories of heaven. . . . We are becoming on this side of the door of death the kind of people we will be on the other side."
—Brian D. McLaren, *A New Kind of Christian*

EXERCISE

Read the Universal Declaration of Human Rights passed by the United Nations General Assembly in Paris on December 10, 1948.[31] The declaration is now seventy-five years old . . .

- If you could take this set of rights that came out in 1948 and add five more rights to the list, what would you add?
- Would you eliminate any of these rights as "outdated"? Would you reword any of the rights listed here?
- Ask yourself, as you read, how these articles are or are not connected to this chapter's theme: compassion.

Note: Women delegates played a key role in speaking up for women's rights as the Universal Declaration of Human Rights was crafted. Hansa Mehta of India is credited with changing the phrase "All men are born free and equal" to "All human beings are born free and equal" (see art. 1). Eleanor Roosevelt was appointed a delegate to the United Nations by President Harry S. Truman. She was elected chair of the commission by its members. She and Hansa Mehta worked together to assert human rights for women.

31. United Nations, "Universal Declaration."

Objective (O)

Impartial, Rational, Unbiased, Deliberate, Curious

Objectivity is a form of intellectual self-discipline and a commitment to truth-seeking honesty. First, we must recognize that each of us has a limited vantage point, a narrow view through a small window based on personal context and experiences. We can gravitate toward a broader and expanded reality by allowing multiple, credible voices to contribute to our "knowing." Doing so allows us to look through a bigger window. Reading and traveling can also play a role.

As a college educator I saw this firsthand. Students would often talk about how encountering required core curriculum classes such as science and math, literature and history, philosophy, geography and political science enhanced their thinking skills and broadened their understanding. Sometimes people who do not have such experiences recognize changes in the outlook of people who do.

When I was in the PhD program in history, one of my favorite uncles asked me if I was still able to talk with him and my other "less educated" relatives who lived in a rural area. I was stumped and stunned by his teasing. How could doing research and knowing more be anything but good? Why would relying only on my own experiences, folding myself into a geographic area, and limiting myself to a familial perspective be a better option? Happily, my uncle and I continued to enjoy each other and joked around a lot. For a time, he took college classes, despite a commute and his responsibilities. We were never alienated from each other. He was a curious person; so was I.

Even though all of us inherit and develop established first principles to build on, people can learn to go beyond a family mindset, cultural tradition, and groupthink. Our point of view evolves from personal experience, study, observation, our work, family, and friends. Objectivity requires a willingness to change our mind and our behavior as information comes to us. As our expertise and knowledge grow, our understanding does too. We learn to refine, question, and correct. We develop analytical skills and expertise. Experience is priceless for researchers partly because they have learned which questions to ask so they can identify a blind alley. The practice of analyzing objectively requires training, discipline, patience, reasoning skills, and repetition. Objectivity also requires the confirmation of other experts.

Who has time for all that? Researchers do. Doctors do. Mechanics do. Teachers do. Expertise is invaluable in every field.

Most people give credit for and admire expertise and the use of an objective approach. The rational approach to discovery builds over time and is never completely "settled." Tender-minded people can be uncomfortable with that, while tough-minded people like to keep at it, even when finding an absolute truth is unlikely.

It is wise for nonexperts to trust seasoned experts who have engaged in long-term, careful research using trusted methodologies. Not appreciating the arduous work and the patience and persistence required for research is a form of cynicism that is unjustifiable. In my area of study (history) it results in incompleteness and/or distortion. Historians are experts who write and tell true stories about real people using written sources that can be evaluated by other historians.[1] Some of what happened is unpleasant, irresponsible, and hard to look at, but we tell the story because it is useful and necessary to understand events and consequences, and because we seek to know what is *true*. Whitewashing history is a grave academic act. Historians may have a specific interest or perspective, but they do not have personal facts.

The consequences of people being distrustful of the expertise of professionals in medicine can be deadly. Sadly, numerous people died of COVID because of fear of vaccines or refusal to admit that COVID exists. Methodology conducted by scholars and evaluated through the peer review process is much better than guesswork or internet surmising. Scholars must go through the peer review process of seasoned experts who will let want-to-be experts know in no uncertain terms if their work is flawed or

1. Hence the footnotes in this treatise. When I wrote my dissertation, I was told not to quote someone in English unless I could read the quotation in the language it was written in to verify the accuracy of the translation. That meant learning some Latin, which really slowed me down!

sloppy. The experts' feedback helps scholars and researchers refine their research—if it is worth refining.[2]

The academic world has strict standards for good reasons. People depend on tough-minded experts for sound research and helpful answers. New answers lead to new questions, more research, more knowledge, more review, and more revision. Tender-minded people may make fun of expertise, glorify common sense, and see tough-minded people as "other."[3] Accepting knowledge that comes from expertise is not only wise but also a form of appreciation for the hard work involved. In short, not all "ideas" are equivalent. Verified "facts" are the result of careful analysis, trial and error, and ongoing research. Answers to complex questions require considerable time, patience, and due diligence. People who seek quick black-and-white answers to complex issues and problems can find those answers only by dismissing evidence and expertise. Some suspicious people doubt "authorities," no matter how carefully the research has been done. Objective people trust reason, research, and expertise to lead the way.

Climate change and the COVID virus have sucked expert climatologists and epidemiologists into a vortex of debate that demeans their expertise and compromises their effectiveness. Sometimes we simply do not want what is true to be true, so we suspend judgment and continue hoping additional research comes out the way we prefer. Sometimes people practice denial until reality (hotter temperatures, hurricanes, melting ice) forces a consensus. It is not unusual to meet vocal people who have no factual knowledge of a topic, yet they are outspoken deniers of the research of experts and the threats we must confront. Climate change research has been verified repeatedly, but some people are climate change deniers anyway. Scaring vulnerable people away from evidence and medically proven help is unkind, as are making up "facts" and spreading falsehoods. Facts cannot simply be selected by way of preference, like personal clothing or "good" food. We cannot simply choose our truths the way we choose a shirt or a detergent. "Alternative" *facts* do not exist. If you identify other people who believe in the same alternate reality as you do, the group thinkers

2. See Reis et al., "Effect of Early Treatment," for an example of research on whether or not ivermectin (used to eliminate parasites like worms in horses) was an effective treatment for COVID. The research method is described. Some people who fear vaccines inject themselves with ivermectin weekly rather than get vaccines. They also use it as a substitute for flu shots. Note: Beware of untested remedies.

3. The phrases "tender minded" and "tough minded" were first used by the American philosopher William James.

you interact with will reinforce your thinking with their own fake fact preferences.

Personal gain goals can lead to a desire for something to be true even when it is not. Suspicious people with a reflex-like distrust of well-educated scientists, educators, journalists, and other authority figures have various motives and reasons. Wishful thinking and sowing doubt against expertise is not objective thinking; it is harmful thinking. People do not like to be told what to do, so it is no surprise that people do not like to be told what to think, even by experts.

Sharing flawed information has never been easier. Groups form around falsehoods easily because internet platforms affirm and empower like-minded people. Was an election really stolen? Does "your" reality depend on which group you belong to or which websites you visit, or is there a reality out there somewhere?

Unfortunately, this is not harmless fun. The anti-authority attitude among people who want to choose "truth" from a buffet of unproven ideas may be less about systematic discovery than it is about dismissing or "owning" the experts. Rather than respect methodical research and inquiry, which can be slow, ongoing, and change with the latest information, too many people turn to unproven fringe hypotheses such as declaring that chemtrails or contrails that we see behind airplanes are spraying the population with harmful substances.[4] Spreading untested and unproven ideas on the internet is harmful, unkind, and irresponsible. Consider how problematic it is to assert that "beliefs" of all sorts should be respected, even untested ones.[5]

A sizable group of people think nothing of leading other people off the cliff. When the blind lead the blind into error, people get hurt. They get sick. They may even die. Society cannot move forward on common goals when we are attacking each other, calling each other names, and being disrespectful of research methodology. The idea that no one should question or challenge your individual "right" to believe what you cannot confirm is a harmful notion. We are all wrong sometimes, but "head in the sand wrong" is a stubborn attachment to an idea or a group that abandons reason, often for the sole purpose of belonging to a group of like-minded people. One should always ask questions and show respect for real research, reputable

4. See Coleman, "Chemtrails."

5. See St. George, "Long Tale."

sources, and expertise. Political or religious ideology is no excuse for denying objective reality.

The internet is both a helpful tool and a source for the dissemination of false information that can pit us against each other. Tribes emerge. Foreign leaders scheme to weaken our institutions by reinforcing fears and spreading lies and division. Connecting with and supporting people who lack expertise and are gullible does not make a false belief true; it makes it dangerous. If you want to say the sky is lime green, or the earth is flat, explain your position using factual evidence. Saying that "I *believe* that it is, and I have a right to do so" is not a convincing position. (People may very well leave you alone, though, if that is your goal.)

The Foundation for Critical Thinking, a nonprofit, publishes a booklet entitled *The Miniature Guide to Critical Thinking Concepts and Tools*. In one section, "The Problem of Egocentric Thinking," a list of five psychological standards that are seen in egocentric thinking is provided.[6] These are: 1*) It is true because* I *believe it*, even though I have never questioned why I do or the basis/source of my beliefs. 2) *It is true because* we *believe it*. The dominant beliefs of my group are true, even though I have never questioned the basis of those beliefs. 3*) It is true because I* want *to believe it*. You believe what "feels good or right" to you and supports your thinking rather than considering the negative argument, because you do not want to change your thinking or admit you are wrong. 4) *It is true because I have* always *believed it*. I want to maintain beliefs that I have long held, even though I have not considered whether current evidence would justify those beliefs. Finally, 5*) It is true because it is* in my interest *to believe it*. People sometimes want to justify personal advantage. For example, areas of the economy impacted by climate change have a financial reason to go slowly and even deny reality.

Objective people take time to examine the positions they hold using these guidelines: 1) What are your first assumptions? 2) What are the sources of your information? With which authority figures and evidence do you associate these ideas? Why do you consider these authority figures trustworthy? 3) What would be the implications if everyone accepted your beliefs or positions? 4) Do you have a purpose or justification for "believing" what you have chosen to believe? Is that purpose noble and beneficial to the common good? Is it in any way self-serving or related to profit or politics?

6. Paul and Elder, *Guide to Critical Thinking*, 6.

Shoddy thinking does not lead people to respect you or even to want to spend time with you. It isolates you from rational, thoughtful people. As you move further out to the fringes, you may become odd or strange with no way of coming back to your original self. You may also become angry. Try holding your ideas in your hand like you would hold a small bird, tenderly, but not so protectively that the bird cannot fly away.

Some of us have lost confidence in our leaders, especially the ones who peddle falsehoods and fear. Must we also lose confidence in the scientific method and rational analysis of facts that experts have devoted themselves to uncovering? Consider how divisive it is for people to choose their own facts. Perhaps we could ignore irrationality and the deniers of reason and science if there were no children to raise, vaccinate, and educate. For their sake, objectivity must prevail. People who are ignorant or dismissive of objective, rational facts may be good people, but they will not be good leaders, and parents are leaders.

Expertise matters in part because extensive knowledge and experience can help a researcher develop intuition about where to search, what to test, what to rule out, and what to study next. Science does not have all the answers, but science has a methodical, systematic way to plod forward toward those answers. Step by step, and by means of rigid precision, a question or problem reveals itself. Flip-flops and mistakes take place, but repetition and collaboration with others undermine going too far down blind alleys toward erroneous information.

When objective people say, "Follow the science," they are not saying that scientists make no mistakes. They are saying that scientific *methodology* can be trusted to identify and correct errors. They are saying that the *methodology* will work if followed. How simplistic it is to dismiss the work of all the experts with a wave of your hand after reading something on the internet or listening to talking heads with ulterior motives! Why not decide not to decide when you do not know enough to take a position. That is what an objective person would do.

We typically accept the expertise of our auto mechanics, our yard service people, trained chefs, designers and contractors, our doctors, our teachers, our meteorologists, and climatologists, knowing that they could be wrong sometimes, but they still know far more than someone who is untrained and less experienced. Let us hope that the people on whose shoulders rests the future of our planet, our health, and the well-being of our children and our neighbors are at the very least rational, smart, and *objective*! That can be the case only if their educators work at reinforcing objective methodology year after year, class after class. Imagine how demoralizing it is for the hardworking people who create medicines and vaccines to fight diseases to have uninformed people suggest home remedies to friends and family, some of which are harmful.

Professional societies develop standards and guidelines that maintain credibility, thus the American Medical Association and the American Bar Association, reputable publishers and newspapers, and academic publications for scholars who engage in methodical research with a critical eye. Good research evidence is expected, respected, and highly valued. What is not expected is that people who have done no research and have no significant information to contribute will just brush aside information they do not like or declare the detailed work of experts to be "fake." In the courtroom, facts matter. Lawyers have ethical and professional standards by which they must abide in a court of law. They cannot simply bluster, whine, or make false claims like a carnival barker. Doing so will get them disbarred. Like science, the courts require evidence, facts, and the testimony of experts and witnesses.

When people turn their backs on what is known to be true because they *wish* it were not true, they are a danger to themselves and others and a hindrance to social progress. Who does not wish we had not faced a pandemic? Who does not wish that we could continue as we have for the last one hundred years in our use of energy sources? But wishing is not facing up to reality; it is stalling, and it is irresponsible.

Historical study teaches us that people are naturally conservative about making changes in their way of life, especially if they expect their income or economic security to suffer. We should expect early resistance to change that requires effort, adjustment, money, and widespread cooperation. Loss is rarely welcomed, so denial is a normal human reaction to unpleasant, rapid, or frightening change. But how can we tackle the problems if we do not acknowledge the problems? How does undermining scholarly research and expertise help us cope? Experts of all sorts deal with reality. None of us gets to "select" a reality (except in video games).

Even so, it is human to initially react negatively to a reality that is too grave or too difficult to accept. When the first person told me that my parents had died in a car accident, I shot back: "That's not true!!!" Denial is a natural reaction to "bad" news. In the *short term*, denial is forgivable. But in the long term, it is a way of avoiding that which is difficult or even dangerous to society and to making progress on difficult issues. Reality does not go away, so we must buck up and come together to do what needs to be done. Making progress together on difficult issues is a form of community building. Objectivity and evidentiary knowledge must be embraced as useful tools if solutions are to be found. We must question and analyze information objectively if the fabric of our society is to be strong rather than ripped apart.

People who have not developed objectivity may be undereducated and ill informed, but they are not "other." They are still our neighbors or part of our family. They may have other admirable traits. They may be quite kind, generous, or creative. We can encourage them by sharing verifiable information. We can praise and promote the work of analytical people.

Sometimes the missing link in people who lack objectivity is curiosity. Without curiosity, probing is shallow or nonexistent. When I taught college, the best students were the curious students who asked questions that allowed me to clarify or go into more depth. People with curiosity challenge easy answers to tough questions. Curious people delve more deeply and explore the works of the experts in the field. The best approach to reality deniers is to thoughtfully engage, without trying to change their minds. (That is unlikely because they have fears and motives.) Interact with people who hold "easy opinions" rather than "facts" by asking questions in a respectful way.

Rather than dismissing someone who tells you that we never went to the moon, politely ask questions rather than showing disdain or walking off. You may not change the person's mind; that is not the point. You interact to show respect for the *person*, not their ideas. You do not have to be an expert yourself. You could ask, Why do you think that? Where did you read that? You could suggest that they visit the NASA website or take a tour of the Kennedy Space Center in Cape Canaveral, Florida. Experience is priceless. Questions and suggestions express curiosity rather than condemnation. You engaged. It *is* worth your time. Engaging helps maintain the strength of our social fabric. Isolating, ignoring, or condemning people who hold ideas that are irrational or unprovable drives people toward a group of people who will agree with them, i.e., unquestioning believers.

People who deny what is accepted by objective people may do so because they enjoy challenging authority. Standing up to the big boys, the educated, and people of different races and genders is a form of sport. It makes some people feel strong or important. Once they connect to a community of like-minded people who reinforce each other, they shut down and circle the wagons. Disagreeing with experts sets them apart from people they differ with on other issues, often political ones. The group members reinforce each other in their fears and their lack of expertise. If you think it is fine for some of us to prefer one truth over another, then you may think each person has the "right" to decide what is true. On this, Daniel Moynihan said it best: "Everyone is entitled to his own opinion, but not his own facts."[7]

Conspiracy theories have become an odd form of entertainment in some groups. People may unquestioningly embrace poorly formed and false ideas because what they really want is not objective truth; they want to play along, have fun, and belong to a community. Fun is fine. But must the political realm entertain us? Must politicians be a source of fun and merriment instead of seasoned, experienced people who want to lead a nation based on a platform of ideas that tells us what they want to do once in office? Have you heard anyone say, "I do not 'like' either candidate, so I am not going to vote"? Elections are not about which candidate you would want to like enough to socialize with. Elections are about a candidate's plans and what a candidate will try to *do*. Elections are not about self-identity and self-expression; elections are about policy, navigating change, keeping people safe, and moving into a planned future that brings with it order, hope, and systemic change in response to challenges.

People are naturally averse to change and want to remain comfortable in the "knowledge" of personally selected or preferred ideas. They are sometimes overly eager to denounce new and disruptive ideas. Using his newly invented telescope, Galileo (d. 1642) presented evidence that physical matter exists in the heavens. People laughed when he brought his telescope to dinner parties. "If there is matter up there, why doesn't it fall? What holds it up? Did you paint the glass?" The consensus at the time was that only weightless light existed in the heavens because anything with mass or weight would fall. Galileo could not answer the questions people asked, but he did not deny *what he saw*. He described it in a book, *The Starry Messenger* (1610). Consequences ensued. He was silenced by religious authorities who did not want the concept of a sun-centered universe to become public, since most people, including church authorities, had built elements of Christianity around an earth-centered universe.

Galileo's insights were admittedly hard to prove or explain. Yet Galileo wanted to tell as many people as possible about what he knew. He wanted

7. Moynihan, "No Easy Answers," para. 2.

other people to *help* him explain what he saw! He published his book in Italian, the language of the people, rather than Latin, the language of scholars, so that *more* people could read it. Seen as a threat, Galileo was censored, imprisoned in his villa near Florence, and forbidden to publish more texts. More evidence was needed, and it came, from Johannes Kepler and Isaac Newton.

People who "rock the boat" are often thrown into the water, sacrificed by people who have a reason to preserve the status quo, make money, maintain power, or control "public opinion." Besides, no one likes to be *wrong*! Evidence is necessary for objectivity and rational analysis, but even evidence is not enough for people who do not *want* to know or do not *want* to change their thinking. The status quo works for them. Profit motives play a part in resistance to change, too, otherwise we would be making more progress on addressing climate change.

Objectivity and rationality require courage. Powerful forces are at work to influence people's thinking, and they have new tools for spreading misinformation. Controlling what people think and think about has become both a source of power and wealth. And yet, "facts do not cease to exist because they are ignored."[8] So let us be courageous and get past our tender-minded rejection of challenging information, the same way people in the seventeenth and eighteenth centuries had to come to terms with a sun-centered rather than an earth-centered universe when the evidence came in. Math and physics explained the three laws of motion, orbiting planets, and gravity. The good news is, the sky did not fall. The church carried on. Christianity survived. We have managed to live with the "new" information and continue exploring to learn more.

Our current challenges are to come to terms with climate change, become better stewards of the earth and its resources, stop the spread of diseases in an increasingly interconnected world, confront and undermine the rise of nationalistic tyranny and nation-state expansion based on the ability to defeat and/or occupy other nation-states, and soften and undermine the stubborn patterns of economic and political injustice and abuse of power that leave people in such despair that they risk life and limb to go *somewhere* other than where they are by accident of their birth.

Because people must *learn* how to think critically, rationally, and objectively, educators have adopted this as a fundamental educational value. In the leadership course I once led we had a segment on "thinking

8. Attributed to Aldous Huxley.

critically." Frankly, people are not prone to it. They do not know how to do it if they are not taught. It requires patience and inquiry and the courage to challenge the falsehoods and distortions that hold us back in our inquiries.

According to neuroscientist David Eagleman, the brain is always busy with analysis of some sort. We use both reason and emotion to reflect on what is good and bad about what happens to us.[9] Both systems are part of our decision-making. Change makes people feel unsafe or scared, and that state of mind makes it easier to manipulate their behavior. Each of us needs to recognize manipulation and the reasons and sources of it. We are rational people, not spineless puppets.

One of the most powerful emotions is anger. Rage and anger can be useful motivators if they lead us to take action to address issues. But manipulators *use* anger to rev people up; they also use fear.[10] Soon no one is thinking rationally or carefully about solving problems that need solving. Have you ever noticed how often political candidates use the verb "fight"? Is an election, a political contest, being confused with a boxing match?!

Typically, the goal of people who distort the truth by fearmongering is to arouse an emotional response that has a mind-body connection. How easy it is to see the powerful physical reaction of an angry person! Angry people have real symptoms, including red faces, a rapid heart rate, and higher blood pressure. They may perspire from exertion. Anger is a form of physical arousal that is *sometimes* useful and motivating, but we must also be aware that anger is *always* useful to manipulators who want to control our thoughts and actions.

Some anti-intellectual newscasters purposely present information designed to evoke an angry reaction that has physiological consequences. The anger flush is exciting. Telling someone off is a form of release. It feels good.[11] *But, it is not a constructive high that leads to positive action.* It is just a feeling, a release of pent-up energy that has no positive outcome. People who want to demonize others, call people names, poke fun at people, and

9. For more analysis of the brain and its curious, diverse ways, see Eagleman, *Brain*.

10. Thomas More was imprisoned by Henry VIII because he refused to recognize the newly created Anglican Church that was to be headed by the king, a secular ruler, not a clergyman. More was starved, threatened, and prodded, but he remained firm. In the film *A Man for All Seasons* (directed by Fred Zinnemann), More's comment to his persecutors was: "They are terrors for children, Master Secretary, not for me!" More was executed for his resistance and is a recognized saint in the Catholic Church. He is the patron saint of lawyers, statesmen, and politicians.

11. Kleuk, "Righteous Indignation and Porn."

arouse anger are selling weak, faulty ideas. In short, they are engaging in what can be called intellectual porn. Some unkind people seek out the hot thrill of being angry. They tend to enjoy condemning and poking fun at people.

While anger can be useful in the form of righteous indignation, humans are rarely objective (rational) and angry (emotional) at the same time. Pay attention to your emotional arousal. Pretend you can step outside yourself and watch your reactions like a disinterested observer. Are you angry because you have been treated unfairly or badly? What or who aroused anger in you and for what purpose? According to Sarah Smarsh, the author of *Heartland: A Memoir of Working Hard and Being Broke in the Richest Country on Earth,* "Anger is a contagious energy that jumps quickly from one person to the next. It will seize your mind and body as its host. If allowed to explode, it will hurt others. If allowed to implode, it will hurt you."[12] Be alert to the words you use. Avoid creating tension and distance from other people. Downplay or avoid what sets you off emotionally. Try to recognize feelings of anger and fear, then hold them up like an object that is separate from you. Think critically about your angry fervor. Were you manipulated by someone with an agenda? In summary, we really need the ability to pause and analyze if we are to function well in a complicated world in which lies have become the tools of people who want to exploit our hopes and fears for their own purposes.

If you feel angry rather than informed, you are being manipulated or played for a purpose. The anger-triggering industry is out to impact people's beliefs and behaviors. The goals are to raise ratings and viewership, increase clicks, and funnel power and money to someone or some group. Provoking anger and fear are the tools manipulators use to acquire and stay in power. Distortions and fabrications have become effective triggers. We do not have to take the bait. Notice how election season ads distort reality to get voters' emotions up, to arouse outrage, rather than to be informative. The goal is to turn us against each other for someone else's political/personal gain. This is our country, our social fabric, and our relationship with fellow citizens. We need to talk through issues that are rightly debatable without relying on dogmatic ideology and unnuanced tribalism.

Maintaining an absolute position on complex issues can be insensitive to the positions or values of other people. Aristotle thought about this. One way to recover from populist anger-driven positions is to recover centrist

12. Smarsh, "Covid Rage," para. 9.

pragmatism, and to do that we must abandon absolute dogmas and find a middle position from which we can work. Rational thought combined with practical wisdom can be useful. Of course, the middle ground may not satisfy absolutist thinkers. Even so, a pragmatically rendered virtue, a.k.a. an *intermediate virtue*, based on allowing the moral agency of others to be considered, is a form of virtue that abandons either/or positions for a higher purpose, *the well-being of the social fabric*, which has multiple threads, colors, and patterns. In short, decent individuals can disagree with other decent individuals, but "laws may not be implemented if they require some members of society to act wickedly or wrongly by their own moral lights."[13]

We will never all agree on what is virtuous and what is not, but we can agree on what is damaging to people and society, because we are witnesses to the *outcomes of practices and policies* that allow this or that behavior. We can *objectively* analyze those outcomes.

Respect for the moral agency of others means acknowledging the limits of ideology and belief systems and having a degree of humility regarding our personal wisdom or our political position. Religious norms, practices, and beliefs will never be uniform in the US. But people of various religious traditions can live next door and develop friendships, even worship together, and try to understand each other without agreeing on all issues. The citizens of the United States must do the same around the political and economic issues and ideologies of the moment. Statesmen and stateswomen need to interact with each other like neighbors, rather than demonizing or avoiding their colleagues or pouting about not getting their way every time a vote is taken. If they cannot do that, a strongman will step up and make the decisions instead.

We cannot simply choose our truths like we choose a restaurant or a detergent. There is no such thing as "alternative" *facts*. By supporting the decency values of the CORTHODOX Way, perhaps political leaders can begin to communicate with and respect each other. That's a start. The alternative could be some form of tyranny.

Soccer or football players can run all over the field, but they still must stay in bounds. Boundaries are set to establish fair play and a degree of order. A free society has norms, laws, and traditions that protect the liberties

13. Fournier, "Ancient Virtue Antidote." See also Douthat, "We Aren't in Vegas." Douthat explores how the pursuit of consistency of policies has led to allowing what is damaging to society to be normalized. Example: Once we had very little access to gambling without traveling to Las Vegas; now gambling is widespread, normal in sports, and used to fund education; and, we have a gambling problem.

of the people. Sometimes those rules restrict and aggravate me, sometimes they restrict and aggravate you, but we can agree to disagree and follow the rules necessary for the well-being of "the game." Societies that function smoothly do not have players who cheat or walk off the field. When we come to expect and enjoy give-and-take reciprocity from various sides of an issue, we are less likely to expect all or nothing, less likely to embrace extreme positions and extreme political candidates and leaders. Winning now and then is rewarding, but not at the expense of the game.

How do you choose objective news sources? A good rule of thumb is to pay attention to the music at the beginning of the program. Is it loud and meant to "get you going" so that you cannot ignore it and will turn your attention to the "emergency" being described? Do you get short pieces of bite-size information in a steady stream intended for people lacking a good attention span for inquiry? Do you have moments of smug agreement about the "insights" paraded before you? Are people, especially females, dressed to keep you watching?

Here is a suggestion: abandon the manipulators. In Megan Garber's article "We've Lost the Plot," Garber writes that reality has become distorted "by our pathological need to be entertained." Dystopian writers have repeatedly warned that we have become entertained by trivia and illusion. Garber says we are so "dazed by our fiction . . . that we'll lose our sense of what is real. . . . The result will be a populace that forgets how to think, how to empathize with one another, even how to govern and be governed."[14]

Try reading the news from multiple sources. Watch the more deliberative newscasts. For example, PBS has no commercials or political ads. You get *an hour* of unrushed content. No one yells at each other to arouse anger. The journalists look more like your neighbors, and they interview experts or people in positions of authority, not just other journalists.

You can supplement credible news sources by reading objective, in-depth, critical journalism in investigative, reputable newspapers and magazines. Always be alert to who is the owner of the "news" you watch or read. Owners often have an agenda to push; they may be "selling" certain topics to gain personal advantage, accomplish political goals, and increase wealth.

Critical analysis does not feed on anger arousal. The goal is to inform, pass on knowledge, and explore the complexity of issues, reasons for concern, and in some cases personal action. When you feel anger and/or

14. Garber, "We've Lost the Plot." See also Goldberg, "Media Challenge Before Us."

self-righteous smugness from watching or listening to a "news" source, you are being manipulated. Be aware of when you are poked and provoked.

With new communication technology (the radio, the television, and the internet), people hoped to be better informed, more aware, and even more unified. We soon found out about the underside of mass communication and the power of broadcast owners to massage, select, and distort information, sometimes even tell lies.[15] Communication technologies are *tools*, like money. They can be used for good and for bad depending on the character of the people using them. *People* are good and bad, not the tools.

Where would Hitler's Nazi movement have been without the radio? After the Germans invented transistor radios, you could stay tuned in to the Führer's rages. (The German *Volksempfaenger* VE 301 radio was introduced in 1933.)

The indiscriminate unsubstantiated allegations of Republican Senator Joe McCarthy were broadcast on a new communication tool, the television. McCarthy's desire for influence, reelection, and popularity drove him to lie when he said that Communists had infiltrated the US government. What if McCarthy had not been confronted about his lies on TV? (His credibility faltered after that interview.) Perhaps he hoped to be president by being the "tough on Communism" guy? Happily, lying to people in the mid-twentieth century was frowned upon and a sign of poor character.

The US Congress asserted a degree of control over radio and television through the Federal Communications Commission. We are still waiting for Congress to exert some degree of regulation over the internet on behalf of both the nation and the public's best interest. We currently live in the Wild West while billionaires rake in money. We regulate to protect. That is why you are driving a safer vehicle than your former relatives. (My parents were in a car with no side door protection when they were killed in a wreck in 1979.)

As for the internet, people bog down in limitless rabbit holes that call people to "come on down." Would the January 6, 2021, insurrection in the US have occurred without the anger-provoking conspiracy theories that spread like wildfire on internet sites?

15. About lies and liars, their reasons, methods, goals, and the consequences, I recommend Scott Peck's book *People of the Lie* and C. S. Lewis's little book *Screwtape Letters*. Peck's description of "evil" is from a psychological point of view. Peck describes his own revulsion of working with people who will not self-criticize to change for the better. They are not motivated to be good, but to *appear* to be good, hence, "people of the lie."

The Reichstag fire in Germany, an incident that Hitler lied about, was used to take control of the government there.[16] The fire in the parliamentary building had not been set by Communists as Hitler asserted; he lied. An investigation later found that the fire was caused by an electrical problem. "Later" did not come soon enough. Hitler became a dictator before the truth about the fire was known. He did not really *want* an objective investigation into the cause of the fire. He wanted to *use* the fire to create hysteria by way of a fake "emergency" (a lie) so he could declare martial law, ban other political parties, and take over the German government.

The lessons of the Third Reich in Germany are useful and wisely learned by every generation: "'Without Hitler, there would have been no Holocaust.' . . . Without thousands of accomplices there *could* have been no Holocaust."[17] Untold numbers of Nazi collaborators were involved. So were untold numbers of ordinary men and women. Hitler was a madman, literally, for he was always throwing temper tantrums. He used his anger, grudges, and manipulation to convince the German people he would bring them glory and victory if they followed his lead. He led them to a hellish defeat. When he realized Germany would lose the war, Hitler gave up on the German fighters in the field as too "weak." Even so, an astonishing number of Germans kept their faith in him. He used them and their affection for their people and their country, as well as their desire for national greatness. Then he created a "staged exit" for himself by initiating an attack on the Western Front during the latter part of World War II. Cruelly, he threw more noticeably younger men at the Allied forces even when he knew the war was over.[18] They need not have died. Hitler used and understood the power of anger. He left Germany defeated, tattered, weary, broken, and divided. *That* is the legacy of a man who promised to make Germany great.

This is a story about what happens when ethical norms are pushed aside, bent, or suspended. This is what happens when rule of law is abandoned for one-man rule. This is what happens when gullible people are hoodwinked by angry speeches and head-in-the-cloud promises. This is what happens when patriotism gives way to racist nationalistic fervor. This is what happens when people close their minds, suspend their reason, and buy into an ideology such as the superiority of one group over all the others.

16. See Miller, "1933 Germany's Democracy."

17. Fritzsche, "Hitler and the Holocaust," para. 8; emphasis in original. First sentence quotes Volker Ulrich.

18. Fritzsche, "Hitler and the Holocaust," para. 9.

People who say "it's just politics" are normalizing lies, manipulation, and cheating. Citizens must hold politicians to the basic standards of decency described in this treatise. One of these is trustworthiness. Trustworthy people do not lie.

People can choose the best leaders only if they are rational, critical, objective, and aware of how their emotions are being played. Ignore the campaign flyers that seek to stir up division and hatred of the "other," or send them back to campaign headquarters with a note of disapproval attached: "You must think I am *stupid* to send me junk like this! I vote for expertise, relevant experience, the ability to unite and lead, and good character."

The English philosopher John Start Mill (d. 1873) wrote about objectivity in his essay "On Liberty":

> The greatest orator, save one, of antiquity, has left it on record that he always studied his adversary's case with as great, if not with still greater, intensity than even his own. What Cicero practiced . . . requires to be imitated by all who study any subject in order to arrive at the truth. . . . if he is equally unable to refute the reasons on the opposite side; if he does not so much as know what they are, he has no ground for preferring either opinion. The rational position for him would be suspension of judgment, and unless he contents himself with that, he is either led by authority, or adopts, like the generality of the world, the side to which he feels most inclination.[19]

Mill advised people to listen to all that is said against them without lowering themselves to attack others. Mill believed a person seeking to influence other people must face criticism with an objective, open mind. Anyone attempting to sell an idea must listen to what is said to the contrary of their position to discern the legitimacy of their own position.

I want to live in this universe!

Objectivity requires mental toughness and rational open-mindedness. If an idea survives scrutiny, it deserves to take its place in the world of ideas. If it does not, or if the owner of the idea is tender-minded and unable to endure or respond to sober-minded criticism and rational debate, the idea must be shelved, not protected.

19. John Stuart Mill, in L. Johnson, "He who knows only," para. 10.

No idea should live on just because someone "likes" it.[20] We cannot become too fragile to be deliberate and objective in seeking the truth. We must see the world for what it is, imagine a better world, and do our part to create it. Spinning our wheels and demeaning each other is not just petty; it is damaging to the social fabric and the strength and survival of democratic government. People who are ignorant or dismissive of objective, rational facts cannot and will not be good leaders.

RELEVANT QUOTES AND TOPICS TO PONDER

- Aristotle argues that *the moral agency of others must be considered* when devising laws. He argued for nuanced differences rather than "absolute" positions. He says that no one or group should be able to impose their "absolute" position on other people. To do so is to disrespect and minimize other people. He believed that rational thought combined with practical wisdom can suggest a useful *middle ground* that may not satisfy absolutist thinkers but creates and sets boundaries that preserve the social fabric. What would a middle position be on gun ownership, abortion, legalized marijuana, and gambling?
- Identify one or more "beliefs" that you think would be problematic if acted upon. What makes a belief deserve our respect and protection?
- Contrast Hitler's speeches with those of Martin Luther King's speeches. What does King say about personal character? Race? Decency?
- According to Steven Johnson, the human life span doubled between 1920 and 2020 as a result of science and activism; pharmaceutical discoveries, including vaccines; and pasteurized milk.[21] To understand how science and activism doubled the human life span, and to recognize the hard work of scientific discoveries in medicine and pharmaceutical breakthroughs, including the history of vaccinations that have saved so many lives for so long, read Johnson's "Living Century." Surprise, surprise! people resisted what came along at every turn, vaccines, pasteurized milk, etc.

20. "Likes" create the algorithm feeds that go to countless accounts, creating pockets of like-minded people who are not exploring the content, just absorbing distortion and manipulation. It does not have to be this way. Read Tarnaff, "More Egalitarian Internet."

21. S. Johnson, "Living Century," 12–13.

- One way we learn is by listening to people tell their stories. As a historian, I have a strong preference for true stories about brave, moral people. Tim Alberta tells Ed McBroom's story beautifully. This story underscores some of the points made in this section and in upcoming sections. It is encouraging. It reminds us to be true to ourselves, to use our good judgment, and to respect the facts. It is also a story of integrity, honesty, and love of country and family. The Republican senator from Michigan, Ed McBroom, is a role model of courage and integrity.[22]

"Hatred is a great motivator, but it burns down more than the object of its ire. You can feel rage but there has to be something on the other side of anger."
—Esau McCaulley, a New Testament professor who commented on Howard Thurman's *Jesus and the Disinherited*

"He who subdues his anger, he who does not regard the bad word of others, he who is not angry even when there is a cause, certainly acquires the four objects for which we live (namely Dharma, Artha, Kama, and Moksha). Between the two men, one performing sacrifices continually every month for one hundred years and one who does not feel any anger, the man who does not feel any anger is the greater man."
—Adi Parva or the Book of the Beginning, one of the first of eighteen books of the Hindu text the *Mahabharata*

"Being offended is the natural consequence of leaving one's home."
—Fran Leibowitz, *Week*, May 18, 2021

"We all depend on other people for much of what we know or believe to be true. So we're all vulnerable to misinformation. . . . Lay people who dissent from the scientific consensus may . . . pride themselves on being independent minded. Still, social delusions pose shared difficulties."
—Kwame Anthony Appiah, *New York Times Magazine*, July 18, 2021

"It is more ominous than any oblivion, to see the world as it is. . . . I don't think there is any greater loneliness than looking directly at the

22. Alberta, "Senator Who Decided."

untamable fury of our world. . . . But it's the only hope we have of finding our way to one another again."
—Carolyn Forché, *Blue Hour*

"To argue with a man who has renounced the use and authority of reason, and whose philosophy consists in holding humanity in contempt, is like administering medicine to the dead, or endeavoring to convert an atheist by scripture."
—Thomas Paine, *The Crisis*

"People often claim to hunger for truth, but seldom like the taste when it's served up."
—George R. R. Martin, *Week*, Nov. 19, 2021

"I've never met a person who would consciously choose to live in captivity. Yet I've witnessed again and again how willingly we hand over our spiritual and mental freedom, choosing to give another person or entity the responsibility of guiding our lives, of choosing for us."
—Edith Eva Eger, *The Choice: Embrace the Possible*

"To think clearly, we must be able to speak freely . . . to disagree intelligently, we must first understand the views of our opponents profoundly . . . to change people's minds, we must be open to the possibility that our minds might be changed. All of this asks us to listen charitably, argue candidly, consider deeply, examine and re-examine everything, above all our own deeply held convictions . . . to respond to ideas we reject with more and better speech, not heckling or censorship. . . . To abandon facts is to abandon freedom. If nothing is true, then no one can criticize power. . . . If nothing is true, then all is spectacle. The biggest wallet pays for the most blinding lights."
—Timothy Snyder, *On Tyranny: Twenty Lessons from the Twentieth Century*

"Some people are inveterate truth seekers. They are almost congenitally willing to risk rejection, ostracism, even hatred for the sake of being right. But most people just want to belong, and the most essential elements of belonging are agreeing and conforming. Would-be belongers engage in what's known as 'preference falsification,' pretending to enjoy

things they don't, or subscribe to ideas they secretly reject. They go along to get along, because the usual emotional companion to intellectual independence isn't pride or self-confidence. It's loneliness and sometimes crippling self-doubt."
—Bret Stephens, *New York Times*, June 2, 2023

"Hate speech is happening in private groups. This is something Facebook launched just a few years ago, this push . . . towards private groups. The idea is that people wanted to be in small, intimate groups with like-minded people. But what happens when those small, intimate groups are QAnon or when they're militias? Everyone is like-minded, and so no one is reporting the content. In some cases, it's not a matter of Facebook's algorithms not finding things. It's a matter of Facebook creating these . . . secluded, private, walled gardens where this kind of talk can happen, where hate speech can happen, and it's not being found."
—Cecilia Kang, in Gross, "Reporters Reveal 'Ugly Truth'"

In *An Ugly Truth: Inside Facebook's Battle for Domination,* by Sheera Frenkel and Cecilia Kang, the authors discuss how Facebook policies declared to be in favor of "free" speech are not for "true" speech.

"We cannot make social media good, because it is fundamentally bad, deep in its very structure. All we can do is hope that it withers away and play our part in helping abandon it."
—Ian Bogost, *Atlantic*, Nov. 10, 2022

"Ideologies . . . keep man in a state of servitude, while claiming to provide him with the best of all possible worlds. . . . [They are] filled with absurd self-contradictions, the greatest of which claims that in order to bring peace to the world nations must be ready at any moment for a war of massive extermination."
—Thomas Merton, *Love and Living*

"Today, a man's ideas of goodness and badness are generally supposed to be matters private to himself. The good life is something to be lived apart from, and often in spite of, the social system of the day. Religion, for instance, is a private affair, a matter for the individual's conscience. To Plato, this division of life into a public and a private sphere was not

to be tolerated. Politics and morals were the same. Bad politics lead to bad behavior."
—E. W. F. Tomlin, *Great Philosophers*

"I think if we want people to genuinely own their mistakes, then you have to offer the possibility of redemption."
—Helen Lewis, *Atlantic*, Aug. 19, 2022

Gustave LeBon (d. 1931) was a French MD and social psychologist who had an interest in anthropology, archaeology, and natural science as well. His books *The Psychology of Peoples* (1894) and *The Crowd* (1895) attributed progress to the intellectual elite who had been taught to think critically and objectively. He thought modern life was too dominated by crowd-like assemblages in which the personality of the individual in a crowd is so submerged and the individual mind is so overwhelmed that the collective crowd mind dominates. LeBon described crowd behavior as unanimous, emotional, and intellectually weak. He writes: "The masses have never thirsted after truth. They turn aside from evidence that is not to their taste, preferring to deify error, if error seduce them. Whoever can supply them with illusions is easily their master; whoever attempts to destroy their illusions is always their victim. An individual in a crowd is a grain of sand amid other grains of sand, which the wind stirs up at will."

"What is needed today is not more leaders . . . but more followers. What is needed are ordinary people: alert, informed, engaged, mobilized, idealistic but not naïve, critical but not hopeless, confident about who they are and what they want *but able and inclined to work with all sorts of others*, exercising rights won at enormous cost, starting with the right to vote. What is needed . . . are more citizens, prepared to lead our leaders."
—James Goodman, *New York Times*, June 29, 2017; emphasis added

"The lack of respect for the science that sets limits for environmental protection is jaw dropping. A plethora of scientific logic was employed to protect our water for all of us. A handful of nonscientists cast these protections aside in a moment. Similarly climate scientists have done extensive research on the changes in our climate. They have made dire

predictions for our future and valuable suggestions to avert some of the problems. Here again a powerful pack of nonscientists blocks whatever action it can. Science should speak to all of us.... Yet, there is a growing trend to dismiss science.... When that dismissal reaches Congress and the Supreme Court, we are all in serious trouble. We desperately need to face the scientific facts about pollution and climate. These issues are already screaming at us in terms of human health and climate stability.
—Sally Courtright, *New York Times*, June 4, 2023

“We have never been more entertained. That is our luxury—and our burden. We have never been able to share so much of ourselves. And, as study after study has shown, we have never felt more alone. Screens are everywhere; the entertainment is so vast, you can get lost in it. . . . The news has become entertainment, and entertainment has become the news. . . . Amusement . . . becomes a means of captivity rather than escape.”
—Megan Garber, *Week*, Feb. 10, 2023

“We can’t run a republic together if we don’t allow our fellow citizens to get things wrong. Becoming estranged over a lapse in political judgment is especially unhelpful. . . . Exchanging ideas is a central part of political participation; it allows us to change one another’s minds.”
—Kwame Anthony Appiah, a.k.a. “The Ethicist”

“We don’t need . . . pushing people to one side or the other. . . . What we need is the dull, factually correct and accurate middle. Because only from that middle will come the solutions. Solutions never come from extremes. . . . You have to recognize the realities of the world and the realities of the world tend to be unpleasant.”
—Vaclav Smil, *New York Times Magazine*, May 1, 2022

“The real problem of humanity is the following: We have Paleolithic emotions, medieval institutions, and godlike technology.”
—Biologist E. O. Wilson, *Week*, Aug. 6, 2021

“Education is a progressive discovery of our own ignorance.”
—Historian Will Durant, *Week*, Sept. 24, 2021

Alarmed by Facebook's crucial role in advancing the cause of authoritarianism in America and around the world, and the lack of a moral compass, "employees pleaded with company leaders to address how its algorithms amplify extremism and misinformation." The employees were ignored. The January 6, 2020, storming of the US Capitol was part of the festering anger . . . Facebook encouraged. Sadly, the Big Lie was possible only due to social media . . .
—Ellen Cushing, "How Facebook Fails 90 Percent of Its Users"

In her article "Collaborators," Anne Applebaum draws from her book *Twilight of Democracy: The Seductive Lure of Authoritarianism*, which has compelling heroes who stand up to authoritarianism. About Wladyshaw Bartoszewski she writes: "He was a leader of the wartime Polish underground, a prisoner of both the Nazis and the Stalinists, and . . . then finally the foreign minister in two Polish democratic governments. Late in his life (age 93) he summed up the philosophy that had guided him . . . . It was not idealism that drove him, or big ideas, he said. It was this: *Warto byc' przyzwoitym*—'I was just trying to be decent.'"
—Anne Applebaum, *Atlantic Magazine*, July/August 2020

Note: Herb Paine, a psychologist, argues that human beings who know little or nothing about a topic often are highly confident that they fully understand and have sufficient knowledge to take a position before they really do. In fact, Paine says we often think we know more when we know very little (he calls this position the Mount of Stupidity). Awareness of complexity and one's own ignorance is often followed by a sinking feeling (despair) as we realize how unenlightened we really are. At that point despair kicks in and we either stay in the valley of despair, or we seek more knowledge and competence, which involves climbing out of being a know-nothing-much-about-this kind of person to someone of competence and enlightenment.[23]

23. See the article and diagram in Paine, "Intellectual Divide."

DISCUSS

- Why do you think human "confidence" is highest when we know *the least* about a subject?
- Why is it wise to respect expertise and scholarship in certain areas rather than "common sense"?
- What is dangerous about oversimplifying complex matters and distrusting expertise?

Responsible (R)

Reliable, Accountable, Deliberate

All of us must make choices and decisions to which we will be held accountable. Decisions and actions have consequences. Living into what we decide and do is an act of responsibility. We are responsible for our mistakes as well, and sometimes those actions cannot be reversed, even with a sincere apology.

A young woman who worked at a bridal shop was delivering a recently fitted bridal gown to the bride. She ran through a stop sign and slammed into my parents' car. My father died at the accident scene; my mother lasted a few hours at the hospital. The young woman who ran into the drivers' side of their car had been driving in an unfamiliar part of town. She told the police that she did not see, expect, or know about the stop sign. Nothing she could do would bring my parents back.

As family members gathered at my home the next day, the doorbell rang. I answered it, but I did not recognize the two people standing there. The young woman who slammed into my parents' car stood there with her mother. The driver had come to say she was sorry. I froze. I had not expected or wanted to see her or even know who she was. She looked like one of my college students. I could not say, "That's OK. You did not mean to" or "Accidents happen. I know you are sorry; let it go." I just stood there, frozen, and said nothing. I nodded to her and closed the door. To this day I wish I had said something kind or forgiving, but I was too shocked and wounded.

Even now, over four decades later, when I see reckless driving, I feel disdain for the driver. I will never feel relaxed or safe on the road. I am hypervigilant. What if I make a mistake that causes someone to be injured or die? What if I become *her*?!! A neighbor of ours in Florida was sentenced to jail following a wreck with injuries, partly because she had been drinking alcohol. Her husband divorced her. I do not know who raised her teenage daughters, but I walked past her empty house often and felt sorry for her, her family, the victim, and the victim's family.

Consider the turmoil of a new high school graduate leaving school to work or attend college. Many new responsibilities mark the end of dependency and the beginning of new personal choices that will have lifelong consequences. Think of the angst of a young couple considering whether to marry or not, have a costly wedding or not, or have a child or not. Maybe some of you know what it feels like to sign the papers for a student loan or a first apartment or a mortgage. These personal decisions are not all irreversible, but they carry with them personal responsibility and accountability. In making such decisions we ask questions and consult with experienced people we trust and admire. We deliberate the pros and cons in an analytical and unbiased way. While we seek out a variety of perspectives, we know that our choices are personal to us because *we* must live into and with the decisions we make. Sometimes we do not know what we want. I wish I had a dollar for every advisee I counseled who changed their major in college. All a new college student can do is imagine what they think they *might* want to be and do. Choosing a course of study is a big decision because it affects your way of life.

A letter written in 1861 by William James, a nineteen-year-old student at Harvard, is telling. James is now known as a great American philosopher/psychologist. But when he was nineteen, his father, a renowned theologian with enough wealth to ensure that his son could get a degree from a prestigious college, strongly encouraged him to study medicine. The young William wrestled with having to make a choice between profit and purpose. His well-off family expected him to study medicine and become a successful, respectable physician. William wanted to marry, and he wanted to ensure that his family had the advantages of a good income (a responsibility that fell primarily on the males of his era).[1] Even so, he was not that set on becoming a doctor, despite the income, prestige, and the encouragement of his parents. Once at college, he wrote a letter to his mother saying he would study science but not medicine. He changed his major to comparative anatomy and physiology.

1. William married Alice Howe Gibbens. They had a long, fruitful, and intimate marriage and were clearly best friends too. They had four children and endured the loss of a fifth.

As a student in that department, he studied under Jeffries Wyman, an anatomy teacher. Wyman is described as "a brilliant yet humble man who imparted on his pupils, by way of personal example, enduring values of kindness, generosity, humility, unflinching integrity, and a resolute refusal to advance himself at anyone else's expense."[2] Wyman had great influence on James, whose description of his beloved teacher's good character follows. It serves as a reminder to all of us to keep trying to be decent, because we are all examples to other people, and our way of being in the world influences the people we encounter.

About Wyman, James wrote:

> His extraordinary effect on all who knew him is to be accounted for by one word, character. Never was a man so absolutely without detractors. The quality which everyone first thinks of in him is his extraordinary modesty, . . . his unfailing geniality and serviceableness, his readiness to confer with and listen to younger men. . . . Next were his integrity and his complete and simple devotion to *objective* truth. These qualities were what gave him such incomparable fairness of judgment in both scientific and worldly matters. . . . He had . . . too little of the ego in his composition, and *all his faults were excesses of virtue.*
>
> A little more restlessness of ambition, and a little more willingness to use other people for his purposes would easily have made him more abundantly productive, and would have greatly increased the sphere of his effectiveness and fame. But his example on us younger men, who had the never-to-be-forgotten advantage of working by his side, would then have been, if not less potent, at least different from what we now remember it; and we prefer to think of him forever as the paragon that he was of goodness, disinterestedness, and single-minded love of the truth.[3]

William James graduated from Harvard with a degree in medicine, meeting his family's expectations. James, too, had "a single-minded love of the truth." He studied philosophy and psychology on his own using the libraries of Harvard and Boston College. He practiced medicine briefly, but his career was in academia. He became a lecturer at Harvard University, focusing on psychology and philosophy. He is renowned for being the first American psychologist and for his role in the philosophical movement known as pragmatism. He suffered with depression, failing eyesight, and

2. Popova, "Choosing Purpose over Profit," para. 9.

3. Popova, "Choosing Purpose over Profit" para. 9; emphasis added.

inadequate income at times. Even so, he found his way between profit and purpose and left a notable legacy.

Like James, I enjoyed school. I loved college. As a college student I was certainly not privileged. I ate a lot of cereal, but I was happy. The quad on the university campus was a secular version of a monastic cloister, the quadrilateral enclosure reserved for those who had taken religious vows. The separation of town and gown at the universities where I studied made the campus feel like a sacred space where I could reflect. If only it had not cost money to continue my education and go to graduate school! If I continued my studies, I would graduate with loans to pay. My parents did not offer to help because I had a younger sister whose "turn" it was to get her degree.

"But what will you *do*?!," asked my friends and family. "Wouldn't it be smarter to study something besides *history*, something more lucrative. Teachers do not make much money, and you are spending a lot of money!" What is "enough" money, I wondered?

The point of these stories about James, myself, and the topic of responsibility, is this: *Your first responsibility is to yourself.* How you make a living, what you need for income, whether to marry and have a family, whether to worship in one tradition rather than another, or not at all, whether to live here rather than there, and how to take care of yourself, these are specific, personal questions to be answered by you. You are responsible for the person you become and the contribution you choose to make. The alternative to living a responsible life is to live a haphazard life, a life that unfolds willy-nilly or purposelessly, or to live into the expectations or hopes other people have for you. You want to be proud of the life you live. You also want to pay the bills and take care of the people you love. These are hard choices that must be made.

Responsible people thoughtfully make their own decisions, and they do their best to live into them. Even when they choose to change direction, a decision that may affect other people, responsible people act with awareness and compassion for the people they may disappoint.

In short, responsible people own their lives and their decisions. They do not live as someone else expects them to live. They consider other people, even in challenging times such as a divorce or a career change. They try to consistently act according to what is good, fair, and right because they think the actions they take, even privately, should be consistent with the values they have for themselves. They take their personal actions seriously.

Responsible people are not perfect, of course. They make mistakes. They learn from adverse experiences, like all of us. They may break a promise they fully intended to keep. They apologize and make amends if they can. Even people with values and good intentions disappoint others and themselves sometimes. All of us count on the forgiveness of others to move past our mistakes and blind spots.

Responsible people do not live as if "I got mine; I hope it works out for you and later generations somehow." Our descendants are counting on us to consider the human community over time. This moral priority is often neglected because too many of us think, "Oh well, I won't be here to face the difficulties or the ire." A lack of concern for the people who live around and after us is irresponsible, a form of self-centeredness and disrespect for others.

Responsible people know that ideas and words can lead people to decide to act, so they consider the various ways their words and actions influence people. Because of the web and social media, our "reach" may be wider than family, friends, and colleagues.

The internet offers people a cloak to hide behind. Reckless, irresponsible people will pass on information without verification. They will say whatever comes to mind and manipulatively foment anger and hatred. Doing so is both irresponsible and unkind. What we may vent about, other people feel a need to "do something" about. For this reason, we must edit ourselves because we are responsible for how our words influence other people.

David French follows the funnel effect in his article about the attack on the Capitol (Jan. 6, 2021).[4] An election loss in 2020 led some people to claim the election was stolen. Angry about that, agitated people adopted a slogan: "Stop the Steal." Blame was recklessly cast. Lies were told and repeated. Action was encouraged. Hard-to-dispute rumors spread about the integrity of the election. Some people showed up in Washington, DC, to protest, attack, and vandalize the Capitol. Gallows were erected; people chanted, "Hang Mike Pence." Threats of violence toward people created mayhem.

After thorough investigations the conclusion is that the election was not stolen.[5] But in the heat of anger, misinformation thrived on the internet, television, and radio, reaching many disappointed people. The angry

4. French, "Truth About Extremism."

5. Reuters Fact Check, "Does 2000 Mules Provide Evidence."

camaraderie of the disappointed and like minded led to an assault that caused injury and death and challenged the validity of the election outcome. The assault on law enforcement officers that day caused injuries for 138 of them. Five people died before, during, or following the events of that day. Terrible consequences, including suicides, resulted. Some of the perpetrators were imprisoned for a time.[6]

Who was responsible for the violence, deaths, and injuries?

A former Facebook employee, Frances Haugen, said that in the days after the 2020 election chaos CEO Mark Zuckerberg temporarily tried to give more weight to quality mainstream news sources, but he soon reverted to the old algorithm that allowed people to spew out election disinformation and other "bad for the world" content that generates emotional engagement by means of angry dopamine hits. So white supremacists can send posts praising hate-filled mass shootings. People fearful of vaccines can spread disinformation that results in illness or death. The Burmese can spread enough hate about the Rohingya to cause a massacre. Teenage girls can swap tips on cutting and starving themselves. All without consequences for the enablers?

Where does responsibility lie? What is the responsibility of Facebook's Mark Zuckerberg to regulate content? If not him, who? How is the damage caused by unchecked postings and advocacy of violent activity like or unlike the court cases that have held Big Tobacco or Purdue Pharmacy accountable for illnesses and deaths?[7]

Throughout your life, situations will unfold and the questions you must ask yourself are these: Where does responsibility lie? What is my responsibility to myself? What is my responsibility to others? In short, what is the responsible thing to do?

RELEVANT QUOTES AND TOPICS TO PONDER

> "A human being's first responsibility is to shake hands with himself."
> —Henry Winkler

6. They were pardoned in 2025 by the president, who respected them and complimented them for their loyalty and service.

7. See Falk, "Editor's Letter."

"In the long run, we shape our lives, and we shape ourselves. The process never ends until we die. And the *choices we make* are ultimately our own responsibility."
—Eleanor Roosevelt, *You Learn by Living: Eleven Keys for a More Fulfilling Life*

"First say to yourself what you would be, then do what you have to do."
—Epictetus, Roman Stoic philosopher

"The best armor of old age is a well spent life preceding it. Life employed in pursuit of useful knowledge, in honorable actions and the practice of virtue; in which he who labors to improve himself from his youth will in age reap the happiest fruits of them; not only because these never leave a man, not even in the extremes of old age; but because a conscience bearing witness that our life was well spent . . . yields an unspeakable comfort to the soul."
—Cicero, Roman statesman

"Character isn't something you were born with and can't change, like your fingerprints. It's something you weren't born with and must take responsibility for forming."
—Jim Rohn

"To be nobody-but-yourself—in a world which is doing its best, night and day to make you everybody else—means to fight the hardest battle which any human being can fight."
—Poet E. E. Cummings, *Week*, Nov. 19, 2021

"Most people do not really want freedom, because freedom involves responsibility, and most people are frightened of responsibility."
—Sigmund Freud, *Civilization and Its Discontents*

"Character—the willingness to accept responsibility for one's own life—is the source from which self-respect springs."
—Joan Didion, *On Self-Respect*

"Optimism is a strategy for making a better future. Because unless you believe that the future can be better, you are unlikely to step up and take responsibility for making it so."
—Noam Chomsky

"It's only when you take responsibility for your life that you discover how powerful you are!"
—Allanah Hunt, *Rebirth: How to Live with Power and Freedom After Separation and Divorce*

"Responsibility is the thing people dread most of all. Yet it is the one thing in the world that develops us, gives us manhood or womanhood fiber."
—Frank Crane

"If feminism means anything, it means taking responsibility for ourselves . . . refusing to be victims."
—Gloria Steinem, *Week*, Jan. 16, 2024

"The nation was not founded solely on the principle of citizen rights. Equally important—though too often not discussed—is the citizen's responsibility."
—John F. Kennedy, "Remarks in Nashville at the 90th Anniversary Convocation of Vanderbilt University, May 18, 1963"

"Responsibility to yourself means refusing to let others do your thinking, talking, and naming for you; it means learning to respect and use your own brains and instincts; hence, grappling with hard work."
—Adrienne Rich, *On Lies, Secrets, and Silence*

Agree or disagree with the following statements. Add a statement of your own.

- Responsible people consider how their actions impact other people.
- Responsible people who borrow from someone pay them back in a timely, systematic manner.
- Responsible people are dependable. They do their best to do what they say they will do when they say they will do it.

- Responsible people own their mistakes. They apologize when they fail someone or act inappropriately. When someone apologizes to them, they offer the forgiveness they would want for themselves.
- Responsible people look after their children. They also take steps to avoid unwanted pregnancies.
- Responsible people take care of property they own or rent. They are not destructive people.
- Responsible people take care of their bodies.
- Responsible people are hope-filled people. They act consistently to create good outcomes.
- Responsible people are truthful people.
- Responsible people do not share other people's stories without permission.
- Responsible people get vaccinated to protect themselves and others.

What would you add to this list? What would you delete? Explain why.

LOOKING AHEAD

- Is it a moral duty, a responsibility, to consider how our actions will affect the people who come after us? Why or why not? Would you agree or disagree that individuals are personally responsible not only for themselves and the people in their lives, but also to future generations?
- Do you think that our descendants will hold us accountable for the impact our current actions have on their future? For what do you anticipate they will blame us or criticize us? Why might they praise us?

Trustworthy (T)

Truthful, Honest, Discerning, Responsible

THE *CORTHODOX* "DECENCY" VIRTUES could *all* be on a list describing *trustworthiness.*

- Trustworthy people are kind and *Compassionate.* They will listen to and empathize with you. They will offer help when they can. Genuine kindness upholds and supports, unlike the self-serving kindness that identifies weaknesses that might be used for personal advantage. Compassionate people will offer what they can without judgment or denunciation.
- Trustworthy people are *Objective* learners who willingly share knowledge and resources rather than holding information tightly for self-benefit. They give credit where credit is due and can be trusted to think analytically. They respect verifiable evidence.
- Trustworthy people are *Responsible* people. They verify information and do not engage in gossip. They can be counted on not to lie or mislead people. They seek answers, value the facts, and purposely build knowledge over time. As a result, people often confide in them and trust them.
- Trustworthy people are *Humble* enough to ask questions, do research, and listen to others. They respect expertise, are not know-it-alls, and avoid making quick assumptions. These traits make them right a lot, which earns them the respect of other people.
- Trustworthy people are *Original,* i.e., they are self-aware. They know their strengths and what they can contribute. They are imaginative, curious, knowledgeable, and inventive. They also acknowledge and

respect the strengths of other people. They work well with others and on teams.

- Trustworthy people are *Disciplined*. They persist when other people might give up. They set goals and steadfastly work toward them. When they make a commitment, they do their best. They live by a chosen set of values and are purposeful about becoming a certain kind of person, so they are both consistent and predictable.
- Trustworthy people are *Open-Minded* enough to know that what they think or know will not always be so. If they get new, convincing information, they willingly revise, or they suspend judgment.
- Trustworthy people are *Xenial* in that they can be present to diverse types of people because they know how to suspend judgment while they listen, and how to first seek to understand.

Trustworthy people know that unity requires accuracy and a shared reality, that people need common facts. An editorial letter of June 2022, by William Falk, the former editor-in-chief of *The Week* magazine, describes various veins of distrust and disunity in the US. Falk succinctly points out that we need to rebuild trust, interconnectedness, and a set of common decency values, particularly *truthfulness*.[1] If lies and exaggerations are protected "free" speech, what protects us from the rancor that results? Developing a disciplined, rational, honest, and inquiring mind and an acceptance of complexity is a good start.

Consider these false assertions:

- Barack Obama was born in Kenya. (He was born in Honolulu.)[2]
- Hillary Clinton was trafficking children in the basement of a Washington, DC, pizza parlor. (A pizza parlor that has no basement.)[3]
- There are secret Democratic cabals of child abusers. (Where?)[4]
- The COVID-19 vaccine implants a method of governmental surveillance into recipients. Vaccines are not good for us; in fact, they harm us. (Experts at Mayo Clinic disagree.[5])

1. Falk, "Editor's Letter."
2. ABC News, "Born in Kenya."
3. Wertheimer, "Fake News Surge."
4. Spring, "US Election 2020."
5. See Mayo Clinic Staff, "Debunking COVID-19 Myths."

- There are millions and millions of undocumented *voters*. ("A new report [by the Brookings Institution] relying on extensive historic data has found instances of voter fraud remain incredibly scarce despite alarm and concern over the potential for such activity to sway the 2024 presidential election.")[6]

We have genuine issues to address. False-flag issues distract, divide, and weaken us. Why are people susceptible to false assertions? Are we less interested in seeking truth than we are in being entertained? Are we mean-spirited in our effort to smear the credibility of our political opponents? Would some of us willingly cheat to win? Who are the snake oil salespeople among us?

Who among us think that selling false and distorted ideas (lies) about political opponents and national decline is fair competition? Why do so many Americans unthinkingly embrace unexamined falsehoods? Who benefits from misleading the public on climate change? Are we being distracted and manipulated by people with something to gain by having us "look over there" while they undermine our unity, destroy our institutions, act in their own interest, and sow distrust among us? Why so much *made-up* fear? Why the willingness to pick and choose our own facts?

People enjoy *belonging to a group* of people, especially people "in the know." Humans have a real need to belong, to find a like-minded group of people they enjoy, but too many people are underinformed, gullible, and overly suspicious of almost everything, including expertise. They believe in and trust only people who share their outrage and distrust, i.e., their own dis-ease.[7] Also, people like to be entertained. Hypothesizing about who is with us or against us is easier than truth seeking, which is laborious and time consuming, so why not have *fun* in a chat room of the like minded?

Today's teachers complain that they are supposed to make learning "fun." Sometimes it is fun; sometimes it is not. Besides trying to meet that expectation, educators must be guarded about *what* they say and *how* they say it, not only in elementary school but in the upper grades, and even in college classes. Why are there so many thin-skinned prickly people eager to be angry at someone and to bully people into being silent? Why so much

6. Aitken, "Voter Fraud," para. 1.

7. McCrummen, "Warrior for the . . . Future."{

sensitivity and fear of exploration?[8] Who is really trying to control what people think, the educators or the people threatened by education?

Politicians try to *rally* us by way of a frenzied outing with like-minded friends. ("Going to the rally will be *fun*!") Political leaders avoid talking about issues facing the nation because to take a stance is to lose a vote. Why alienate anyone? Stirring up rancor and divisiveness and turning people against one another is so much easier, never mind that it rips at the fabric of our republic. The message is "Trust us, not them! *They* are not trustworthy."

Talking about specifics can be politically costly, so what do we hear instead? "Trust *me* to be on your side, to be your hero and protector." People like being entertained more than they like being informed. Why read about complex issues when we can be amused or angry? Political debates are like a wrestling match! After every debate people weigh in on who "won." Some voters may just decide who they "like" the most. People often say they vote for who they "like" more than they vote for experience, a platform, or competence. (This reminds me of what people do online; they "like" this, or they "like" that.)

Unfortunately, even news shows try to entertain us and capture our attention. They open with loud frenetic music; newscasters talk fast as if our attention spans are short, and they must keep us revved up so that we keep listening because we bore easily. Female newscasters dress to keep people watching as much as listening. The news "show" one chooses to watch has become an "identity" for some people, like how teenagers select their favorite music and bands, the clothes they wear, and the food they eat to define themselves and distinguish themselves from their peers.

What if we all insisted on valid information and specific plans? What if we were less cynical and more curious, less politically tribal and more community minded? What if we pondered the common welfare rather than how a proposal helps or hurts *me* and *my* party? What if we stopped blindly following undisciplined liars, entertainers, and manipulators and took the time to read, inquire, and be directly engaged rather than passively

8. Academic life was not, for me, a descent into unquestioned liberalism. I taught college for four decades after having gone to college for ten years. We were not brainwashed; we were encouraged to think for ourselves. I had *one* teacher, a democratic socialist, who was out of the mainstream. He was interesting, but I would be surprised if he changed anyone's mind. He just set a personal example. He was so much more disciplined than we were! He was certainly not a conspicuous consumer! He wore one of two pairs of trousers and one of three shirts to every class all term. (I know this because one of the students made a chart of his rotation!)

manipulated? What if people who run for high office must first have served in the public sector in some capacity so that "the public" has had the opportunity to validate their sense of service and their character? What if we refused to elect people who stir the anger pot because we are, as the Pledge of Allegiance says, committed "to the flag of the United States of America, and to the Republic for which it stands, one nation under God, *indivisible*, with Liberty and Justice for all" (emphasis added)?

We need trustworthy truth seekers with empathy and compassion "for all." If we want sounder policies, less stress and division, and better leadership, it is up to us to demand it and to disconnect from manipulative people who seek to stir up our emotions, provide shallow entertainment, or "serve" in office to benefit themselves.

In an opinion article for the *New York Times* Ezra Klein writes:

> One reason I left Twitter [now X] long ago is that I noticed that it was a kind of machine for destroying trust. It binds you to the like-minded but cuts you from those with whom you have even modest disagreements. There is a reason that Twitter's rise was conducive to politics of revolution and reaction rather than of liberalism and conservatism. If you are there too often, seeing the side of humanity it serves up, it is easy to come to think that everything must be burned down.[9]

What does it mean to be "trustworthy"? In the academic world research is valued only if the sources are respected, legitimate, and properly cited. (Choices must be made regarding valuable sources and weaker sources.) Scholars are taught to read their sources in the language in which they were first written before citing them in English so that the scholars who follow them will know which sources were used and how they were translated or interpreted. Without this strict standard, a scholar's work may be discounted or ignored and their reputation soiled. All relevant information is to be considered. Sometimes questions are raised but unanswered so that other scholars are challenged to continue the search. These scholarly norms bring up the topic of media choices.

Many of the quotations used in this treatise come from subscriptions I have with sources that I trust. Some critics will say that my sources are biased, limited, too conservative or too liberal. This labeling is an attempt to dismiss my work, to assert that I have no discernment or no mind of my

9. Klein, "Chief Ideologist"; para. 26; emphasis added.

own, as if I cannot read something, analyze it, and dismiss it. No one can read everything, so everyone must select the sources they trust. How?

I do not ignore expertise. I am aware that knowledgeable people and diverse sources may vary in outlook. I do not feel controlled by that. When I choose my routine reading material, I ask myself this: If I were graduating from graduate school with a degree in journalism and looking for a position, what would be the most prestigious journals, newspapers, or media outlets to work for? Could I get a job there?

For example, the *Atlantic Magazine*, founded in 1857, is among the oldest magazines in the country. Top-notch writers and journalists are featured on a variety of topics. Some of the main articles are quite long and detailed. It is not aimed at people with an eighth-grade reading level. If some people label this magazine "liberal" or "conservative," it does not bother me. Why? *Because I have sufficient discernment to read a magazine article without being brainwashed by it.* By reading other magazines, like *The Week*, which has short articles from a multitude of sources, I can refine my intake and be exposed to varying points of view. The short articles on all sorts of topics can guide you to other publications and related articles that feature a variety of positions.

One consistent approach to being discerning about what you read is this: oversimplification is a form of manipulation. Sure, busy people find summation helpful, but what and how much is missing? What is the expertise and experience of the authors?

Mature readers avoid oversimplified information sources because they are not trustworthy. Ever notice how many people complain about ads during election season? The ads are so dumbed down and so transparently manipulative that they are off putting rather than helpful. It is wise to avoid any news source that works to get an emotional reaction, *particularly anger*, and to be aware of media stars who seek to divide "the people." Media celebrities who stoke resentment and bitterness are not working for us. They are working against us. Some media sources are self-centered self-promoters working to benefit themselves, politically and financially. In short, they are not trustworthy.[10]

People who target reputable sources as "off limits" are participating in the culture war strategy of controlling what one is "allowed" to encounter

10. National Public Radio and public television news do not allow political ads, and they are not owned by one family or a group in which the primary interest is profit. If you are looking for a source to do some of your fact checking and analysis of stories, visit https://mediabiasfactcheck.com.

and "allowed" to think. We are not children. We do not need to be guarded from information that could be upsetting, incomplete, or biased. Most people recognize when manipulators make efforts to enrage and motivate people. Wise people choose what they read based on credibility. Reading time is precious in our busy world, so selecting quality material written by trusted sources is wise.

Discerning people both accept and reject what they read. They do not need to be told that conservatives read this newspaper and liberals another newspaper or that conservatives watch this channel and liberals watch another channel. Such efforts at control are an attempt to shut people off from information and each other. To what end? Or more importantly, to whose advantage?

We must dismiss and disregard manipulative illusions and seek truth to recover mutual trust. Lies are dangerous, divisive, and manipulative. In his book *People of the Lie*, M. Scott Peck connects lies and liars to evil. Read the book before you decide to dismiss his premise.

Trustworthy people are honest, truthful, sincere, informed, and dependable. These are also the traits of good leaders and responsible citizens determined to get along well enough to create a future worthy of our history and tradition and those who fought for freedom. When these character values are underdeveloped and underappreciated, ethical rot sets in, which undermines our personal lives, our society, and our country.

Step back from the drama. Consider which part you will play in the current era and the future. May it be based on reality, hope, community, and trustworthy people.

RELEVANT QUOTES AND TOPICS TO PONDER

- What do you think you might add to or delete from this list? (This list is printed on a *New York Times* sweatshirt.)

  The truth is hard.
  The truth is hidden.
  The truth must be pursued.
  The truth is hard to hear.
  The truth is rarely simple.
  The truth isn't so obvious.
  The truth is necessary.
  The truth can't be glossed over.

The truth has no agenda.
The truth can't be manufactured.
The truth doesn't take sides.
The truth isn't red or blue.
The truth is hard to accept.
The truth pulls no punches.
The truth is powerful.
The truth is under attack.
The truth is worth defending.
The truth requires taking a stand.
The truth is more important now than ever.

- Do you agree, or disagree, that many citizens have become so accustomed to being entertained and stimulated that the serious business of our era has been reduced to snippets of information compiled to keep us agitated and/or entertained? To what end? Cite a specific article, program, or action as evidence of your position. Explain why you agree or disagree.

- According to Jonah Goldberg, who once worked at Fox, "Most Fox hosts are utterly shameless in their lying, which is why I quit the network. . . . Not incidentally, I often heard these propagandists say one thing . . . in my presence and another thing when the cameras and microphones were flipped on."[11]

  What might motivate newscasters to lie? What do money and power have to do with the "news"? Are they just "readers," or do people look to them to be trustworthy too? How might we ensure that the news we absorb is well researched and unbiased?

- What does it mean to "trust" the "science"?

> Do not trust people who, in their handling of complex questions with imperfect data, manufacture simplistic answers with perfect confidence. Instead, trust people who allow for complexity and uncertainty. Trust people who change their mind when the evidence changes. Trust people who . . . say "Believe the science!," which is the dynamic reevaluation of complicated truths, rather than SCIENCE, in weird caps-lock font.[12]

11. *Week*, "Fox," para. 2.
12. Thompson, "Still Arguing About Masks," final para.

- Why is there so much ideological apartheid on the climate change issue, which British Prime Minister Boris Johnson referred to as "one minute to midnight on the doomsday clock"?[13] How and why did this issue become so divisive if science is increasingly conclusive about the problem?

- Discuss the differences and similarities between *faith*, *reason*, and *trust*.

  Thomas Aquinas would argue that *both* faith and reason are trustworthy ways of knowing. His vision calls for a balance: reason illuminates the natural world, while faith reveals the divine truths that reason cannot fully grasp. What do you rely on as sources of knowing? Why did you choose these sources?

- If you are looking for a source to do some fact checking and analysis of stories, visit https://mediabiasfactcheck.com.

- Denver Riggleman, a former Republican congressman from Virginia, warned his colleagues that the QAnon conspiracy theory was dangerous. On Oct. 2, 2020, he was one of only two Republicans in the chamber to speak in favor of a resolution denouncing QAnon.[14] In his book *Bigfoot: It's Complicated*, which includes an account of an outing he took to find Bigfoot, Mr. Riggleman, a freshman congressman at the time he spoke on the house floor, recounts his experience with fringe ideas and how people are manipulated by false ideas for both power and money.

After questioning the "secret truths" of the mysterious QAnon (whose followers believe that a satanic network of child molesters runs the Democratic Party), he received death threats. He was called a traitor. He lost his GOP primary race the following June. He has been a target and a curious observer of the power secret ideas and stories have on people. Some of his colleagues told Riggleman that QAnon is a "helpful little lie" that cannot be challenged without making the president angry enough to hurt you in the next election. Riggleman was advised to at least pretend to believe the lie, or he would be seen as a poor team player.

If you were Riggleman, what would you do?

13. Higgins, "British Prime Minister," para. 5.

14. Peters, "One Republican's Lonely Fight."

"If the people cannot trust their government to do the job for which it exists—to protect them and to promote their common welfare—all else is lost."
—Barack Obama, "An Honest Government, A Hopeful Future—University of Nairobi," Aug. 28, 2006

"Authoritarians don't want to control just the government, the economy and the military. They want to control the truth. Truth has its own authority, an authority a strongman must defeat at least in the minds of his followers, convincing them to abandon fact, standards of verification, critical thinking and all the rest. Such people become a standing army awaiting their next command."
—Rebecca Solnit, *New York Times*, Jan. 9, 2022

"Imagine taking off all the deceptions and distortions as if they were a cloak around you, being completely clear and honest and giving up control of the outcome of situations. . . .

"Shedding the skin of deception is a courageous step in the journey of becoming unstuck. . . . It brings clarity and freedom to your inner world. What a blessing to keep company with another person who is deeply honest—to trust that he or she will say if they are upset, keep agreements, own their part in a situation, talk openly about their lives, admit to mistakes, and be kind."
—Carlotte Kasl, *If the Buddha Got Stuck*

"Democracy is based on trust in strangers and a sense of having something in common with them, which is part of why xenophobia and fear of crime serve fascist agendas so well."
—Rebecca Solnit, *Week*, Dec. 13, 2024

"All I have seen teaches me to trust the Creator for all I have not seen."
—Ralph Waldo Emerson, "Immortality"

Humble (H)

Grateful, Forgiving of Self and Others

Few people set out to be humble. Successful? Knowledgeable? Helpful? Kind? Generous? Perhaps.

Humble can be confused with being meek, and meekness is confused with weakness. A better synonym might be gentle, as in a person who considers carefully before they talk or state a position. A humble person is one who is still willing to learn, can pass over an argument, and may feel less need to convince others that his or her position is the "right" one. Humility is more about not *needing* to talk, control, demand, or even assert a position. One can be humble and rich, humble and powerful, humble and knowledgeable, and like Jesus on the cross, humble and persecuted. (He even prayed that his persecutors be forgiven.)

Having a positive view of oneself or a low view of oneself are more psychological terms used to describe self-esteem, self-confidence, and the ability to be appropriately assertive. In religious terms we are all both sinners and saints. God loves us anyway. Our relationship with God is not quite the same as our relationship with each other, but humility is essential to both relationships, because people who are blinded by ego and have a sense of superiority (including self-righteousness) are less likely to see their need for either spiritual growth or the human community.

Healthy humility allows us to engage in trial and error. A person may work very hard at something but still be able to "let go" of achieving excellence without personal disdain or dissatisfaction. Being free to try hard and be mediocre, or even fail, allows one to experiment and experience more of life.[1]

1. Don't take up tennis (or other new sports) at age forty plus if you are not prepared to be humbled!

Humility allows us to reach excellence. Notice the dancer, the athlete, the musician. The most talented among us have worked hard enough so that they can forget themselves. If you have ever seen a very talented musician, dancer, or athlete when they are "in the zone," you will notice that look, that absence of ego, the way their performance seems to just pass through them. They forget themselves for a time or become absent to themselves. This is also true of people who have a mystical spiritual experience. Well-known mystics include St. Teresa of Avila, Julian of Norwich, St. Paul, Ignatius Loyola, and Evelyn Underhill (1875–1941), a British mystic, theologian, and author.[2]

Humility allows us to be more genuine with ourselves and more forgiving of others. Without a sense of humility and fallibility, we can become unbearably smug, even arrogant. We may even come to think of ourselves as irreproachable. Know-it-all people are both unattractive and self-isolating; their arrogance, even when they are intellectually outstanding, is unbecoming. But is humility an overcorrection? Is it too much self-denigration?

Micah 6:8 of the Old Testament says, "What does the Lord require of you but to do justice and to love kindness, and to walk humbly with your God?" Of course, being humble before God is easier than being humble before flawed human beings. But Jesus was persistently humble. He served, healed, taught, and comforted those who would listen. When he ministered to poor, sick, and disadvantaged people, he noted that it was the poor and powerless who would find his message more acceptable than the rich and powerful. He suffered through a public execution between two criminals, yet even his last words and acts showed concern for others, including his mother and one of the criminals hanging alongside him. Remarkably, he condemned no one for his brutal crucifixion.

Humble people have a modest view of self-importance and a recognition of their dependence on God, the necessity of being forgiven, and the need to pay it forward by forgiving and serving other people. A degree of humility is required to submit to God's will, to serve other people selflessly, and to become our better selves.

Humility is often contrasted with pride, which is considered the root of numerous sins and the basis of arrogance, an off-putting trait that hardens the heart against service to others who may be deemed flawed or inferior. According to 1 Peter 5:5–6, "God resists the proud, but gives grace to the

2. For Underhill's writings and more information, see Kari, "Evelyn Underhill." Underhill describes mysticism beautifully.

humble." In the Old Testament, humility is expected too. Isaiah 66:1–2 says: "But on this one will I look: On him who is poor and of a contrite spirit." Matthew 7:1 says, "Be not judges of others, and you will not be judged," which is another way of saying, "Do to others as you would have them do to you" (Matthew 7:12).

Sometimes wealthy people feel and act superior because they live differently from other people. People who are intellectually gifted may consider themselves superior for their knowledge and insights. Males may feel superior to females; they are typically bigger and stronger. Youthful people may feel superior to elderly people; they do not suffer limitations, and they are at the beginning while the elderly are near the end. Whom do you know who displays some form of prideful one-upmanship? How do you regard them? Do you find them deserving, admirable, or aggravating?

Buddhists place a strong emphasis on humility. Their tradition teaches that when humility is lacking, it is impossible to live a devout spiritual life. Buddhists regard our lives as fleeting and impermanent. Like a bubble on the tip of a crashing wave in the ocean, people are short lived and imperfect. An abundance of ego and/or personal pride means that a person has not come to terms with their imperfections and their impermanence. In Buddhism, people who exhibit self-importance are unenlightened. Enlightenment requires an awareness and acceptance of our imperfections and our short-lived existence.

One of the most basic rituals practiced in Buddhism is bowing. People bow to show respect to other people, but they do not equate humility with humiliation. In 2009, Barack Obama bowed deeply (at the waist) when he greeted the Japanese emperor Akihito. Uninformed critics made comments about his spineless groveling and argued that his behavior was a sign of weakness. Other people who understood the tradition in Buddhist countries realized that his bow, in this situation, was a show of respect. The bow is a physical way of expressing a spiritual exchange. With the bow, one graciously recognizes the unique importance of another human being in the universe.

Without humility, the ego is allowed to take over. When people practice humility together, no one can claim to be superior.[3] A person who lacks humility may feel justified in whatever he or she says and does, even when it hurts another person. A prideful person may decide they are exceptional in

3. O'Brien, "Principle of Dependent Origination"; Lam, "Being Humble."

their understanding and wise in their actions, so wise and carefully thought out that they are above reproach, blameless, and free of error or guilt.

Ghandi, a Hindu who studied Buddhism, Islam, and Christianity, said that his life was his message, as are all our lives. He practiced humility and wrote as follows:

> Only a little thought will suffice to convince us, that all creatures are nothing more than a mere atom in this universe. Our existence as embodied beings is purely momentary; what are a hundred years in eternity? But if we shatter the chains of egotism, and are melted in the ocean of humanity, we share its dignity. To feel that we are something is to set up a barrier between God and ourselves. To cease feeling that we are something is to become one with God. A drop in the ocean partakes of the greatness of its parent, although it is unconscious of it. But it is dried up, as soon as it enters upon an existence independent of the ocean. We do not exaggerate when we say that life is a mere bubble.[4]

One of early Christianity's teachings on humility is summarized in the Beatitudes, of which there are two versions in the New Testament, one in Matthew (ch. 5) and the other in Luke (ch. 8). Matthew has eight beatitudes; Luke has five. Both sets are challengingly countercultural.

By blessing the poor, the hungry, the meek, and the mistreated, Jesus upends the values common to secular culture, which prioritizes wealth, plenty, prestige, and power.

Matthew's text varies from Luke's text because he uses the term "poor in spirit" rather than "poor." He makes no direct reference to rich people, and he does not mention wealth or poverty. The difference in wording raises a question: What does it mean to be "poor in spirit"? Perhaps it means to be humble.[5]

Blessing people for their humility is somewhat different than blessing people for being poor. Certainly poverty is a source of vulnerability, and having less does make people feel "less than" people whose needs and desires are met. In short, Matthew's summary carries a different message, and it raises questions: Is humility a virtue common to all good, decent people? How is it expressed?

Because we share our communities, countries, and our natural world with people who talk differently, think differently, worship differently, are

4. Gandhi, "Gita and Satyagraha," s.v. "Humility."

5. Roos, "8 Beatitudes."

multiracial, and have different histories, we have learned to practice a patient tolerance as a way of showing respect to people we do not understand, people who are "other" to us. Seeking to understand is a form of humility.

What's the alternative to this? Political absolutism that enforces one faith tradition or ideology over another? A society held together by force, fear, and some form of one-upmanship or zealotry?

Thanks to social media and the politics of grievance, some of us have become angry and disgusted by secular society. We may even want to impose order on the chaos, perhaps some version of the republic of Gilead (a totalitarian, patriarchal theocracy described in Margaret Atwood's book *The Handmaid's Tale* and the media spin-off, *The Handmaid's Tale* series). Among the primary attributes of Gilead's leaders is prideful intolerance and arrogant superiority.

People who decide that they alone know what is true and good are not humble; they are arrogant, controlling, and inflexible. When someone asserts that they are self-righteously peddling the "truth," maybe what they really seek is submission, power, and control. Simply put, they want their way. Cult leaders present themselves as uniquely in the know, inspired, and capable of leading other people to some form of utopia. Stay away from that briar patch!

Charles Baker, the former governor of Massachusetts, liked to quote Phil 2:3: "Do nothing out of selfish ambition or vain conceit, rather in humility value others above yourself." According to Baker, "Insight and knowledge come from curiosity and humility. . . . Snap judgments about people or ideas are fueled by arrogance and conceit. They create blind spots and missed opportunities." "Governing," he says, "as opposed to demagogy, is about earning others' trust and cooperation. Exhibiting a willingness to listen and to hear them goes a long way toward that." Baker continues, saying: "People don't like being accused, people don't like being condemned, people don't like being alienated. It's a matter of conversation and persuasion."[6]

Frank Bruni sums up the role humility can play this way: "While grievance blows our concerns out of proportion, humility puts them in perspective. While grievance reduces the people with whom we disagree to caricature, humility acknowledges that they're every bit as complex as we are—with as much of a stake in creating a more perfect union."[7]

6. Zwelling, "Humility Is the Antidote," para. 8.

7. Bruni, "Most Important Thing," para. 12.

Humility is widely celebrated throughout the Christian tradition. Saint Augustine is said to have written: "Should you ask me, 'What is the first thing in religion?' I should reply, the first, second and third thing—nay, all—is humility. . . . It was pride that changed angels into devils; it is humility that makes men as angels."

Pride is sometimes considered the common denominator of all the sins. And yet, it comes so naturally! We are proud when we achieve success at reaching a long-term goal, when we watch our children evolve in skill and awareness, when we teach and see someone's face light up by a newly perceived understanding. Feeling pride in our own accomplishments and the accomplishments of loved ones is a satisfying feeling, a reward for hard work. But *pridefulness* is distinct. Pridefulness is a form of excessive and habitual pride that manifests as arrogance and/or disdainfulness for others.

One of my favorite Christian authors, Thomas Merton, describes humility as liberation and a form of personal freedom. He is said to have written, "A humble man can do great things with an uncommon perfection because he is no longer concerned about accidentals, like his own interests and his own reputation, and therefore, he no longer needs to waste his efforts in defending them." He says, "Pride makes us artificial, and humility makes us real." Pride can lead to arrogance; humility can lead to openness of heart and mind.

Humility involves being less self-centered and less self-conscious. This openness feels liberating. Maybe you feel it when you experience the vastness and beauty of creation. When you are the least ego centered and selfless, perhaps you can focus on other people and praise their work, talent, insights and gifts without comparing and contrasting yourself to them.

When you silently rock your newborn and your heart fills up with awareness of the miracle and the magic of creation, you glean something about humility. My sister feels liberated from her workaday self when she dances. Some people feel a loss of self-consciousness in prayer or liturgy, in music, in being creative, or when absorbed in their interests or talents.

Sometimes people must crash into some form of brokenness to realize that humility is not a weakness but a strength. Humble people are more open to serving. Humble people develop less ego, so they worry less about how they are perceived by other people. They are free to "follow their bliss." Humble people are calmer; they can lean into listening and resist doing a lot of "telling." Humble people enjoy a freedom, an openness, to God, to other people, to the joys of service rather than the egocentric perks of dominance. As people age, their need for power, control, being "right," and earning strokes that feed the ego slips away. Age and frailty lead to some form of dependence. Humility replaces our need to control, which must eventually give way. Humility is a form of freedom and openness that frees us from posturing and allows us to become our true selves.

RELEVANT QUOTES AND TOPICS TO PONDER

- A sign in a day care center read: "Everyone poops. It's okay to poop." Having a body is one thing we all share. When it comes to experiencing humility, if life does not lead us to it, the body likely will. Discuss the role of the body in teaching us about humility.

"Humility is the root, mother, nurse, foundation, and bond of all virtue."
—John Chrysostom

"The very first step in nonviolence is that we cultivate in our daily life . . . truthfulness, humility, tolerance, loving kindness."
—Mahatma Gandhi, *The Mind of Mahatma Gandhi*

"Pride is the great parent of all the other sins. All the rest . . . greed, gluttony, sloth, lust, envy, anger are rooted in pride."
—Kenneth Swanson, *Enter the Kingdom*

"Let us be a little humble; let us think that the truth may not perhaps be entirely with us. Let us co-operate with others; let us, even when we do not appreciate what others say, respect their views and their ways."
—Jawaharlal Nehru, speech at the Science Congress, Calcutta, Jan. 14, 1957

"The beloved of the Almighty are the rich who have the humility of the poor."
—Saadi Shirazi, thirteenth-century Persian poet

In Islam, humbleness is the opposite of pride and a sign of good morals. Allah said: "That abode of the Hereafter We grant it to those who do not seek to exalt themselves in the earth or to cause corruption in it."
—Surah Qasas 82

"If I have seen further it is by standing on the shoulders of Giants."
—Isaac Newton, letter to Robert Hooke, Feb. 5, 1675

"'You get humbled by life in one second.' If you are lucky, the terrible thing that surprises you is something you can survive."
—Albert Brooks, *Atlantic*, Apr. 29, 2024

"The ascent of identity politics and the influence of social media . . . were better at inflaming us than uniting us. They promote a self-obsession at odds with community, civility, comity, and compromise."
—Frank Bruni, *New York Times*, Apr. 20, 2024

"If Jesus is the revelation of what is going on inside the eternal God (Colossians 1:15), which is the core of the Christian faith, then we are forced to conclude that God is very humble. That is amazing, difficult to imagine. Sometimes I think I could just stop and meditate on that."
—Richard Rohr with John Bookser Feister, *Jesus' Plan for a New World: The Sermon on the Mount*

"Humility is not a weak and timid quality; it must be carefully distinguished from a groveling spirit. . . . We may have honest pride and self-respect . . . though we may be servants we need not be servile."
—Edwin Hubbel Chapin, a Universalist minister and editor of *Christian Leade*r

On August 4, 1944, when the Gestapo burst into the home where Anne Frank's Jewish family was hiding, they stole silverware and a menorah but left the family's papers and Anne's diary on the floor. Anne's biographer, Ernst Schnabel, wrote: "Her voice was preserved out of the millions that were silenced, this voice no louder than a child's whisper. . . . It has outlasted the shouts of the murderers and soared above the voices of time."
—Ernst Schnabel, *The Footsteps of Anne Frank*

"With great passion can come great intolerance. Small differences create big arguments, and then the way in which people argue becomes

more important than what they argue about. . . . Are our differences so great that they justify destroying relationships or institutions . . . ?"
—David French, *New York Times,* Sept. 22, 2024

Original (O)

Creative, Confident, Assertive, Eager to Contribute

Consider the "to be" verb and the phrase "I am." When God is asked by Moses "Who are you?," the reply is "I am the great I am" (Exod 3:14). Assume for a moment that we are all made in the image of God, as the Judeo-Christian tradition says. Assume each of us has a real chance to decide who we will become. How will we complete this statement: "I am . . ."

Although every one of us is influenced by a confluence of powerful forces such as family, nationality, gender, experiences, and social and religious norms, these are not absolute determinates. Each one of us has some choices to make, even when the range of options for us is limited. The question is this: Given my gifts and circumstances, who will I become, and how will I give of myself to the larger world? What will I make of myself? Yes, we all have context to deal with, gifts and handicaps. However, these are not the "deciders" of our lives; we are.

Stoic philosophy emphasizes that it is *on you* to decide how you will be present in a world that is both beautiful and brutal. Those who live life fully choose who they will *be*. They accept the consequences of their choices. (This may have little or no relationship to what they *do* for a living.) They resist having someone else decide their fundamental values for them. They seek the freedom to create a life for themselves, and they accept the consequences of their choices. They do not give up on becoming their best selves, to "live fully" with integrity.

> Suppose someone standing by a clear, sweet spring were to curse it: it just keeps right on bringing drinkable water bubbling up to the surface. Even if he throws mud or dung in it, before long the spring disperses the dirt and washes it out, leaving no stain. So how are you to have the equivalent of an ever-flowing spring? . . .

> Preserve your self-reliance at every hour, and your kindness, simplicity, and morality.[1]

Albert Einstein's biographer wrote that the most important aspect of Einstein's personality was his willingness to be a nonconformist: "He bristled at all forms of tyranny over free minds, from Nazism to Stalinism to McCarthyism. Einstein's fundamental creed was that freedom was the lifeblood of creativity." About this, Einstein wrote: "The development of science and the creative activities of the spirit requires a freedom that consists in the independence of thought from the restrictions of authoritarian and social prejudice."[2] People with originality are curious and imaginative. Einstein was both, and he bravely left Nazi Germany to live where independence of thought was encouraged and respected. After he came to the US, he lived a large, influential life.

Even if not everyone can flee hate and fear for freedom, everyone can take part in promoting freedom wherever they are. The freedom to express oneself, create oneself, assert oneself, and contribute to humanity in some way is essential to a good life. When rules, laws, religions, autocrats, and tradition inhibit people from being their best selves, the loss is a loss for all humanity. Sadly, the "Free World" is quite small. It is primarily a Western world creation that has been difficult to export and costly to protect.[3]

Human beings are a powerful force in the world. We are the only species capable of using our ingenuity and empathy to protect other species. We are also the only species capable of destroying the world we live in. We have gifts, duties, and freedoms.

One of our strengths is our imagination. We can imagine what might be, not just cope with what is. We have invented tools of every sort to enhance our understanding of life and the world/universe in which we live: microscopes, cameras, speakers, satellites, X-rays, night vision goggles, microphones . . . the list goes on and on and belongs to biologists, anthropologists, geologists, geographers, astronomers, foresters, medical researchers . . . every field has its inventions, discoveries, and contributions to

1. Popova, "Stoic Key to Kindness," para. 3.

2. Isaacson, *Einstein,* 550.

3. See Slezkine, "Free World," for an elaboration of what the Free World was and is. The term was coined in the post–World War II era when fascism and communism were fought against and/or resisted. Challenges to freedom come from a variety of sources, and those sources change. They are not always foreign threats. Fear of the "other" has led to intolerant, far-right movements inside countries that were once part of the Free World.

understanding. We need professional, committed newscasters, storytellers, artists, and musicians to empower us. Who will you *be*? What will you *do*?

We have invented weapons to destroy our world, and a way of life that cannot be perpetuated without causing great harm to our planet. Each of us is responsible for what comes next, and we will need smart, creative people with a love for humanity and creation to inspire us and produce ideas, large and small. I am not speaking primarily of political and intellectual leaders; I am speaking of every individual's capacity to salvage or destroy our world and create a sustainable way of life. Responsible people offer their gifts; they play a part.

Decent people are not destructive people. Decent people consider the impact of their way of life on others. Even wealthy people are rightly expected to live with discipline, despite their ability to afford to consume increasingly more, more, more. Yes, everyone matters, for we are all takers; so, it is fitting that we also be givers of ourselves. Perhaps your contribution will be through acting, music, art, dance, song, or storytelling. Perhaps you will teach, protect, volunteer in accordance with your empathy and strengths, and use your resources to empower people who share your values. Your way of being in the world will be up to you. Destroyer or sustainer? Taker or contributor? Kind or self-centered? Responsible or irresponsible? Socrates's phrase "Know thyself" is pertinent here, for you are a co-creator of yourself. You are responsible, within your setting, for who you become and the impact your life will have.

Sometimes what the individual works toward requires other people and more time and patience than are first imagined. Rarely are great and good outcomes the result of one person's actions over one lifetime, so be humble enough to avoid self-focused success or heroism. It is enough to play your part.

Two decades ago, scientists said they had mapped the human genome; they had sequenced 92 percent of it. In 2022, the other 8 percent was mapped. This effort took place over many years and involved numerous people. The cooperative outcome is stunning and ongoing. Having the full code will lead to personalized medicine being tailored to a patient's genetic makeup. We will find out more about aging, infections, and how to survive diseases. With the new knowledge, doctors implanted electrodes in the spines of three paralyzed men. Within hours, all of them could stand, walk, and pedal. This procedure was not *one* person's brilliant idea. It involved the ongoing work of committed people, creative, imaginative, disciplined people.

In short, progress is typically the result of teamwork, not individual heroism, so this section is not meant to imply that you should set out to do important things so that you are personally honored in some egocentric way. It took years, billions of dollars, and over twenty thousand engineers, astronomers, technicians, and government officials to create the James Webb Space Telescope in 2022. Now we can see Jupiter in detail and scrutinize other planets and stars.[4]

You are unique and original. You get to decide which of your gifts you will cultivate for good and what your legacy will be, if not in the larger world, in the smaller world you occupy. This is not a power to be ignored or wasted. We need you, and you need all of us.

RELEVANT QUOTES AND TOPICS TO PONDER

Sometimes a career will begin with an observation that pulls a person forward by curiosity. Einstein wondered what made the needle of the compass move. What were the causal invisible forces at play? He devoted his life to finding out.

People who have an interest and a purpose are either in search of discovery or in the process of some sort of creation. They persist without being frantic. They do not see obstacles as threats; they see them as opportunities to learn more and enhance their understanding. They love the process as much as the product. After all, effort means you care about something meaningful.

Some discipline is typically involved, but people often become motivated and committed when doing something that comes to define them.[5]

- What is the relationship between freedom, individualism, and creativity?
- Often people who accept or engage in repression of some degree or variety argue that conformity of thought and deed is "safer" for society and more comfortable than freedom. Why might they make this argument?

4. Greenfieldboyce, "Why Some Astronomers Feared."
5. See D. Brooks, "Surprising Route."

- Do you have a turbulent soul like Dostoyevsky? This is a list of five resolutions Arthur Brooks uses to guide himself. They could work for you too. Or use them as you like and write your own five goals.

1. My goals in life are mere intentions, not attachments. I will focus on the struggle, the journey.
2. "Conformity of thought and deed is more comfortable than freedom. But I will question everything and think and act for myself."
3. I will turn away the narcotic snares of tech distraction that steal my time and attention in exchange for my freedom of thought.
4. I will embrace the anguish that freedom and individuality bring, because I demand the right to experience love.
5. The world as I see it is not all that exists, nor does it explain all things. I will embrace the transcendental as I seek to understand.[6]

- In his "Letter from the Birmingham Jail," Martin Luther King cited the theologian Reinhold Niebuhr, who wrote that "groups tend to be more immoral than individuals." Does group thinking cause people to commit acts together that they would never commit otherwise? Discuss your experiences with group thinking

"The only freedom which deserves the name is that of pursuing our own good, in our own way, so long as we do not attempt to deprive others of theirs, or impede their efforts to obtain it."
—John Stuart Mill, "Of the Liberty of Thought and Discussion"

"We shall lead in that degree to which we build a vital and healthy society. . . . By demonstrating the limitless powers of a free society which knows how to liberate the full creative energy of man, we shall fulfill the destiny that history has assigned us. . . . My definition of a free society is a society where it is safe to be unpopular."
—Adlai E. Stevenson Jr., speech in Detroit, Oct. 7, 1952

6. A. Brooks, "Fyodor Dostoyevsky's Five Principles," quoting Dostoyevsky.

"He is free who knows how to keep in his own hands the power to decide, at each step, the course of his life, and who lives in a society which does not block the exercise of that power."
—Salvador de Madariaga

"Every human being is intended to have a character of his own; to be what no other is and to do what no other can do."
—William Ellery Channing

"Free will is not the liberty to do whatever one likes, but the power of doing whatever one sees ought to be done, even in the very face of otherwise overwhelming impulse."
—George Macdonald, *Miracles of Our Lord*

"It is better to create than to be learned; creating is the true essence of life."
—Barthold Georg Niebuhr[7]

"We all have different gifts, so we all have different ways of saying to the world who we are."
—Fred Rogers, *You Are Special*

"The most important relationship we can all have is the one you have with yourself; the most important journey you can take is one of self-discovery. To know yourself, you must spend time with yourself, you must not be afraid to be alone."
—Idea attributed to Aristotle

"True happiness comes from gaining insight and growing into your best possible self. Otherwise, all you're having is immediate gratification pleasure, which is fleeting and doesn't grow you as a person."
—Idea attributed to Aristotle

"This I believe: that the free, exploring mind of the individual human is the most valuable thing in the world. And this I would fight for; the freedom of the mind to take any direction it wishes, undirected. And

7. See also http://mercercognitivepsychology.pbworks.com. This site includes resources to help you explore how to develop and unleash creativity.

this I must fight against any idea, religion, or government which limits or destroys the individual. . . . I will fight against it to preserve the one thing that separates us from uncreative beasts."
—John Steinbeck, *East of Eden*

"Always be a first-rate version of yourself, instead of a second-rate version of somebody else."
—Judy Garland

Disciplined (D)

Persistent, Systematic, Goal Centered, Hopeful, Steadfast

THIS CHAPTER IS NOT about your diet, your New Year's resolution to exercise, or your pledge to go to bed earlier, so relax. It is about deciding who you are, who you want to become, and having the discipline to live into becoming your best self.

Socrates reduced the purpose of life to two words: "Know yourself." This maxim was inscribed on the temple of Apollo at Delphi.[1] But knowing yourself is a challenge. Thinking rationally and objectively is not the only way we think. We need to be aware of not just what we think but why we think it, because action follows thought.

How we think and why we do what we do remain a mystery under study. Kent Keith, author of *Monkey Brain*, and Dr. David Eagleman, who wrote *Incognito: The Secret Lives of the Brain*, remind each of us that the conscious you, the "awake" you, that is relying on your intellect to direct your actions, is not always in charge. If you have ever "argued" with yourself, you have experienced this dichotomy.

Monkey brain is described as a subconscious construct in your brain that issues primal directives about survival, comfort, acceptance, power, greed, and identity. These directives compete for dominance. The consequence? No one is always rational, disciplined, and in control. No one.

Let's say you try to walk every day, but today it is super cold outside! Monkey brain kicks in and warns you: "You'll freeze to death! No walking today!" Such thoughts come from the comfort-loving, survival-seeking monkey brain, until you use your discipline-imposing intellect to override

1. The two other maxims there are "Surety brings ruin" and "Nothing to excess."

the programming. You must firmly insist that walking is not optional.[2] In short, the monkey brain can be overruled . . . with effort.[3]

The discipline of rerouting undesirable neuro pathways is why comfort habits are so hard to change! Once you start changing a pattern of behavior, expect to lose the argument with the monkey brain sometimes, but know that your brain has plasticity, and over time your intellect can be a tool for rerouting neural programs. This means that we can be more deliberate in harnessing our reaction to change, that we do not have to do what we have always done or think the way we have always thought. We can be disciplined, objective, and rational, but doing so may *seem* unnatural.

Perhaps the use of the term "monkey brain" disturbs you, even though you are aware of how our minds "jump around" erratically. William Irvine, author of *A Guide to the Good Life: The Ancient Art of Stoic Joy,* uses the phrase "my other self": "he who wants nothing more than to be comfortable and to take advantage of whatever opportunities for pleasure present themselves." The "other" self (i.e., the monkey brain) lacks discipline and is a simple-minded pleasure seeker. According to Irvine:

> My other self is not my friend; to the contrary, he is best regarded "as an enemy lying in wait." . . . I must establish dominance over him . . . to gain self-discipline. And why is self-discipline worth possessing? Because those who possess it can determine what they do with their life. Those who lack self-discipline will have the path they take through life determined by someone or something else, . . . and as a result, there is a real danger that they will mislive.[4]

The Stoic philosopher Seneca reminds us that having endured something difficult or having worked toward something that fell short of what you wanted has a personal payoff even if the *outcome* of your actions was somewhat disappointing. Your efforts could open a way through to a solution you did not anticipate when the baton you carried for a time is passed to someone else whose actions complete what you started. In short, hope must not die because the outcome fell short of what we wanted.

Rather than pinning who we are and what we do for good on a particular outcome, we can focus on simply deciding how we will *be* in this

2. Keith, "Mensa Brain or Monkey Brain?"

3. Mental illness and addiction are challenging precisely because they go beyond the "monkey brain" we all work to control and thwart at times. Discipline is helpful but insufficient for addicts and the mentally ill.

4. Irvine, *Guide to Good Life,* 262–63.

world. We can choose to live as beautifully as we can, with purpose, love, kindness, wisdom, persistence, and discipline instead of despair, hatred, anger, or a nonchalant me-centeredness. We can focus less on the outcome we desire and more on the possibility that our efforts may or may not be in vain in the end. Disciplined people live in accordance with their *values*, so disappointment does not have to become despair. Our life will be well lived if we live a disciplined life built around chosen, meaningful values. Of course we are hopeful about possible outcomes, but we recognize our inability to "make" things happen a certain way.

In summary, disciplined people systematically and steadfastly live a certain way because they have selected and committed to being a certain kind of person, *regardless* of hoped-for outcomes. Our center of self-empowerment is in selecting our goals and values, for the key to living a good life is to value what is genuinely valuable and to be indifferent to what lacks value.

Deciding who you want to be begins by recognizing the traits and characteristics you want to choose for yourself. Consider the traits of people you admire and people you respect. Consider the value or outcome of each trait. What you respect in others and what you adopt for yourself will lead to self-respect when you commit to consistently living by these values. Use multiple sources in selecting the attributes you choose to value. You can be a "disciple" of many admirable people.

By assigning value to attributes that are useful to us *and* to society at large (perhaps the nine CORTHODOX decency values?), we can curb our arrogance and appetites. We can rise above pleasure and pain, control our tempers, and avoid despair. You will also know when to apologize for aberrant behavior that conflicts with your values. Thinking that "Everyone behaves badly sometimes, so what?" is not enough. Disciplined people who fall short of their own values regroup and apologize for behaving in a way that is inconsistent with those values.

Brian McLaren suggests that steadfastly becoming the person you have chosen to be is a powerful source of personal authority, despite the disappointments that occur along the way.[5] When we act, hope, and persevere without focusing on outcomes, we are being true to ourselves while maintaining the hope of the "possibilists." Possibilists argue that even small acts matter, that your acts and the acts of other people can add up to large consequences. You may not know the effect of a small kindness, a smile,

5. McLaren, "Love Is Stronger."

an act of helpfulness, or a simple compliment. You may not know the outcomes of your disciplined behaviors in the short run. You are just being the person you have decided to be.

Young people who are not jaded by disappointment play a large role in keeping hope alive. They are forward looking, passionate, and eager to shape the world they will inhabit for the better. They persist. The option of giving up seems strange, not normal. They are confident that their actions will create a better future despite the cynical reactions of less hope-filled people.

Jane Goodall, an ethologist, conservationist, United Nations Messenger of Peace, and founder of the Jane Goodall Institute turned ninety in February 2024. She marked her birthday that year by continuing to spread her message of hope through action with scheduled events in North America, Africa, Asia, Australia, and Europe. She has co-written a book with Douglas Abrams. Dr. Goodall outlines the four things that give her hope: the human intellect, the resilience of nature, the power of young people, and the "indomitable" human spirit. Goodall writes:

> My definition of hope isn't just sitting and saying, "Oh, I'm sure things will work out." It's like a very dark tunnel full of obstacles, but right at the end, there's that little light gleaming. And in order to get to that little light, you're just going to have to fight to get there. It wouldn't just happen unless you make the effort.
>
> Young people are my great reason for hope. They're passionate. They're not going to give up. They know there's going to be a better future because they say, "By golly, we're all going to make it so . . ." They are . . . planting trees, they're clearing trash, they're raising money for quake victims or hurricane victims or for animal shelters or for some consequential project like saving koalas and looking after them after the fires.[6]

Hope is more of an active state than a passive one. Hope requires discipline, foresight, and, most of the time, teamwork. Hope evolves from setting goals, owning your own agency, and tenaciously struggling toward the goals you set. That is the definition of a disciplined life. Adversity is involved. Flexibility is necessary. Yet the best antidote to despair is a disciplined pursuit of hope-filled-on-purpose action based on long-term, tested values, some of which are described in this treatise. The sources for these

6. Jane Goodall Institute, "Environmental Icon."

values stretch across time, religions, philosophies, and an awareness of the historic consequences that occur when these values are ignored.

Everyone's actions matter. Ancient Egyptian art depicts a scale that was used to weigh the heart of a deceased person. It tipped either one way or the other, and if it did not tip toward the good, the heart was thrown to a jackal, and the deceased person did not acquire the opportunity to experience the great adventure of immortality. By acknowledging that we all have a responsibility to our place and time, we accept our place in the unfolding of consequences. Every day every one of us makes an impact on the people around us. You get to decide what kind of difference you want to make.

You have probably heard it said that "nothing is as powerful as a good example." The Ukrainian people who have fought so bravely against takeover and tyranny have shown us what it really means to believe in freedom and human rights. Their effort is hope and discipline in action. Theirs is a David/Goliath situation. There is nothing ethereal about their action, rather, this is a desperate, bloody, muddy battle for something both fragile and precious to them, their homeland and their freedom. Happily, they have reminded us of our own noble inheritance and made the bickering of the political left and right seem silly, self-serving, and naïve.

Some angry people willingly consider tyranny as a resolution to political division and unrest. But true patriots are not loyal to this person or that person or this school of thought or that school of thought. True patriots love their homeland, and they work to strengthen it for the next generation; they are not devotees of *this* party or *that* candidate. They are not *for* "these people" and *against* "those" people. They are for all "the people."

Provocateurs of anger are not our friends; they are a menace. The anger spewed by political adversaries who behave as if politics is a form of war brings up the relationship between living a disciplined life and succumbing to destructive energy. We have all experienced anger or wrath. Yet anger is not to be dismissed because it is common; it is one of the seven deadly sins.[7] In the end, anger is just a feeling. A disciplined person knows this and makes every effort to manage and examine the source of the anger and to

7. The seven deadly sins are 1) vainglory or pride, 2) greed or covetousness, 3) lust (see the lyrics to Taylor Swift's song "Illicit Affairs" to explore this one and the lies required), 4) envy, 5) *wrath or anger*, 6) sloth, and 7) gluttony (which is usually understood to include drunkenness, not just food). Exploration of these sins can be found in medieval Catholic tradition and in the works of Thomas Aquinas's *Summa Theologica*, Dante's *Divine Comedy*, and Chaucer's *Canterbury Tales*.

practice self-control. With purposeful effort, you can learn how to let anger go through you rather than nursing it.

One model for acting rather than reacting can be found in Mark 5. Jesus was in a synagogue on the Sabbath. A man with a withered arm was there too. The Pharisees who were present did not want Jesus to heal the man; to do so would violate the Sabbath law. Mark says that Jesus looked upon their position with anger, but he did not get into an argument; he healed the man's arm. His action was his teaching. By healing the man, he was teaching that people are more important than legalisms or rules.

In the Sermon on the Mount in Matt 5:21, Jesus says not to "nurse" anger against others. Don't harbor your anger, practice self-examining, forgiving, or coming back around to an issue after you have settled down. In Eph 4:26 Paul admonishes Christians that nursing anger over time can lead to sin and leave a loophole for the devil. He warns that even overnight can be too long. Anger divides, undermines, and disrupts. Everyone gets angry, partly because everyone is bruised, hurt, or disappointed at some point. But anger should be dealt with, some people would say "before the sun sets," in other words, as soon as you can, because anger can be harmful, debilitating, and self-destructive.

Nurturing anger can cause physical injury to oneself. If angry despair is allowed to seethe and simmer, it is likely to erupt, sometimes unexpectedly. Anger that lingers over time can cause a feeling of helplessness or depression and sometimes suicide. Anger can also divide, tribalize, damage society, and lead to violence. Maya Angelou writes: "I can become quite angry and burning in anger, but I have never been bitter. Bitterness is a corrosive, terrible acid. It just eats you and makes you sick."[8]

A disciplined person develops a way to release anger and practice forgiveness. One way is to recognize that anger is a common, ordinary reaction that should dissipate quickly. It may be helpful to picture anger as a dark cloud that passes through you and over you, heading somewhere else.

Try rerouting your anger into positive action. Do something. Address a recurring issue in yourself or in the world. While there is no single way to do this, a very good way is to practice forgiveness. Abraham Lincoln said, "I have always found that mercy bears richer fruits than strict justice."[9] Forgiveness may have to come slowly, particularly if you are hurt by someone you love. That's okay. Your goal is peacefulness, and inner peace follows

8. Chen, "12 Quotes," quote 2.

9. See https://www.brainyquote.com/quotes/abraham_lincoln_133231.

forgiveness. These two, peace and complete forgiveness, are like twins. They hang out together a lot.

Victor Frankl and Elie Wiesel, both Jews who suffered in German concentration camps during World War II, chose to react to cruelty with kindness as a way of setting themselves free. Even amid entrapment and discomforts of all sorts, they felt liberated because they did not allow themselves to become enslaved to anger. Anger ties us to other people and to a situation. Overcoming it takes self-discipline and, for some of us, prayer. The reward is a form of freedom. Wiesel describes the inner person each of us crafts for ourselves as "a universe with its own secrets, with its own treasures, with its own sources of anguish, and with some measure of triumph."[10] (I love this quote! It reminds me who is in charge.)

Disciplined people have a "largeness" of sorts. They have created in themselves a center that guides their actions. They have selected time-honored values and developed a form of wisdom, courage, and confidence. Louis Zamperini, an Olympian athlete and soldier in World War II, was in a plane crash in the Pacific Ocean in 1943. He drifted on a life raft for forty-seven days. He expected to die, but he was captured and sent to a Japanese POW camp.

After his release, he embraced the idea of forgiveness as a form of discipline. He argued that hatred and anger toward another person is like a boomerang that misses its target and comes back to hit you in the head, and that the one who hates is the one who hurts.[11] I wish for you, dear reader, this largeness and the peace that comes with it.

RELEVANT QUOTES AND TOPICS TO PONDER

- Today psychologists help people confront their anger and deal with displacement of anger. Read Golden, "Displaced Anger" (and other articles you find helpful), and discuss how much damage anger can cause, both personally and between individuals. Do you know someone who always seems angry? What do you observe?
- One way to avoid getting into angry conflicts is to learn to be assertive. Become aware of how to communicate and behave assertively so that conflicts occur less often. When you express yourself and feel heard

10. Rhoades, "35 Elie Wiesel Quotes," quote 32.

11. Fuller, "'Unbroken' Story."

you are less likely to stockpile angry feelings because you feel "run over" by some people.[12]

- Write some general rules of conduct for yourself. List no more than ten, and fewer if you see overlap. Share your list with five people, then refine your list. Feel free to revise them. Post your rules of conduct where you can read them every day, perhaps the inside of your closet door. You are typically alone there, and you can make a discipline of reviewing them (and the nine CORTHODOX values from the chart at the end of this book) every time you dress.
- Humans have a way of distracting themselves with consumption. Most people's idea about "enough" is "just a little more, please." How much do entertainment, shallow pleasure, and self-indulgence get in the way of you living a richer, more meaningful life? Consider your norms. What is your life "about"? What would you add to your life to enrich it?
- "Service to others" need not be complicated or overly self-sacrificing. The me-centered mind is easy to abandon once you discover the experience and rewards of being supportive, kind, and helpful to other people. What might you do this week to please or assist someone else?
- When interacting with other people, begin by listening without judgment and realizing that each person is on a journey that is not exactly like your journey. Notice the people you avoid. What are the traits that rub you the wrong way? Ask yourself why you prefer to avoid them. Is doing so unkind or okay?
- A rule of life seeks to respond to two questions: Who do I want to be? How do I want to live? . . . or the interplay between these two questions: *How do I want to live so I can be who I want to be?* How do you answer these two questions? You may find Louis Zamperini inspiring.[13]

12. *Psychology Today* Staff, "Assertiveness."

13. See https://www.azquotes.com/author/19546-Louis_Zamperini.

"If you are not consciously building your habits, they are unconsciously building you."
—Anika J. Green, *Week*, Feb. 17, 2023

"Even if we lose hope for a good outcome, we need not lose hope of being good people . . . courageous, wise, kind, loving, in defiance of all that is bad around us. . . . Hope is complicated. But even if hope fails, something bigger can replace it, and that is love."
—Brian McLaren, Center for Action and Contemplation, May 14, 2024

"Hope is like a path in the countryside. Originally, there is nothing—but as people walk this way again and again, a path appears."
—Lu Xun, *Week*, June 21, 2024

"He who is devoid of the power to forgive is devoid of the power to love. There is some good in the worst of us and some evil in the best of us."
—Martin Luther King Jr., *A Gift of Love*

"To forgive is to set a prisoner free and discover that prisoner was you."
—Attributed to Lewis B. Smedes, a former professor of theology at Fuller Seminary

"The one who forgives never brings up the past to that person's face. When you forgive, it's like it never happened. True forgiveness is complete and total."
—Louis Zamperini, *Devil at My Heels*

"When a person can't find a deep sense of meaning, they distract themselves with pleasure. Pleasure in itself cannot give our existence meaning."
—Viktor E. Frankl, *Man's Search for Meaning*

"Hope is an . . . alternative to the certainty of both optimists and pessimists. Optimists think it will all be fine without our involvement; pessimists take the opposite position; both excuse themselves from acting. It's the belief that what we do matters even though how and when it may matter, who and what it may impact, are not things we can know

beforehand. We may not, in fact, know afterward either, but they matter all the same, and history is full of people whose influence was most powerful after they were gone."
—Rebecca Solnit, *Hope in the Dark: Untold Histories, Wild Possibilities*

"We must all suffer one of two things: the pain of discipline or the pain of regret or disappointment."
—Jim Rohn, Facebook post, Oct. 13, 2015

Open Minded (O)

Listens Openly, Questions, Reads Widely

Openness to new information, useful change, and making a habit of checking one's own objectivity is a fountain of youth for people. We need not *decide* what we think is true once and for all. We need not lose our mental agility as we age simply because we once chose or decided our position at some point along the way. We can re-choose when more information is available. We can take a position *and* continue to live with a degree of ambiguity. Maintaining our curiosity and taking in information objectively, even if it conflicts with ideas formed long ago, is a sign of resilience. Saying "I'm not sure about 'this or that' yet, so I am choosing to suspend judgment" allows us to maintain the open-mindedness to decide later or not to decide at all.

Many people consider being faithful to a set of beliefs as the same thing as being faithful to God. They seek to preserve long-held meaningful traditions and historic value systems, partly out of fear of inviting change with unknown consequences. We all have cherished beliefs, and we all hold firm against abandoning some of them. Replacing or refining a belief might have unknown consequences, both good and bad. No wonder it is tempting to become intellectually settled! Sometimes we maintain our chosen beliefs as a sort of faithfulness to family, tradition, and personal identity. Some people regard what they have previously decided as some form of "common sense." What do you think are the pros and cons to that sort of "faithfulness"?

All of us know someone who refuses to budge on one or more issues. People who have settled in may refuse to *read* anything that contradicts their thinking! It can be annoying and off putting to converse with people about topics we are trying to understand and clarify when other people are overly certain and closed minded. Being open minded means that we are willing to question, consider, and sometimes change our minds.

In Zen Buddhism the willingness to entertain doubt amid certainty is called "beginner's mind" or *shoshin*. Beginner's mind practitioners, like young children learning so much so fast, do not question everything they learn every minute of every day. (That would be exhausting!) You can practice *shoshin* by conversing with people with whom you know you have disagreement. Do not correct that person's statements or positions. Let go of that need. Simply be curious about what they have to say. It does not matter who is right and who is wrong; what matters is who is curious. "Hmmm," you may think, "she or he looks at that differently from me."[1] Avoid an argument by remembering that everyone learns information from someone, somewhere, at some time. Practice realizing the various influences on your thinking, and consider asking about the influences on the thinking of the person with whom you are engaging. Beginner's mind is a form of humility, a recognition that we live in a large mysterious universe and that what is known or normally practiced is not what must always be.

People who study astronomy and physics talk about *multiple* universes. It is impossible to have a small mind and explore astronomy! Check out just one example, the Herbig-Haro 211 images made possible by the James Webb Space Telescope.[2] HH211 is *one thousand light-years away* from Earth in the constellation of Perseus. When our sun was a few tens of thousands of years old, it would have looked a lot like HH211. When you look at HH211 you are looking at an "infant" sun that is in mass only about 8 percent of our sun, but it will eventually grow into a star like our sun and be about the same size. (And you thought the Buddhist notion that we are as small as a drop of water on top of an ocean wave was humbling!)[3]

We do not build roads the way the Romans once did, but we learned a lot about building roads and bridges from the Romans. In the same way,

1. Practicing beginner's mind was invaluable to me when I taught world history to a diverse group of college students who came from a variety of places. Controversial topics would come up, especially when we were discussing religious and political history, the two hot-button topics that dominate history! I learned not to contradict. I asked questions instead. I made a note to come back around to a topic later if I thought it was necessary to correct inaccuracies. That gave me a chance to gather and check information. Many times, I simply said, "Your take and experiences are interesting." They were.

2. Herbig-Haro objects are formed by gas that spews from newborn stars that collide with dust and gas.

3. See https://www.esa.int/ESA_Multimedia/Images/2023/09.

our understanding of what is and what must be true should be held gently. Ethical and moral norms, which are typically rooted in the past, emerge and shift over time. Some people consider faithfulness to tradition, particularly religious and cultural traditions, virtuous and wise. Sometimes it is, sometimes it is not. Fidelity to the past can become an idol of sorts.

Take notice of the modification of roles and contributions people have open to them in different places and in different eras. Males have historically been dominant in history since people started farming, settled down, could own private land, and had to defend their place and possessions from marauders. Women farmed and raised families. Both women and men were living day to day. We know about them from their tools. They were unable to read and could not write their stories. Roles were set by biology and necessity.

As it turns out, women have a variety of gifts to offer in the public sphere. They are often very disciplined students. Yet in many areas of work, women were not expected to lead. (That would mean abandoning the "idea" that men are "natural" leaders and not meant to be led by women.) I remember when women were treated as if they were grown-up "girls," like Lucy and Ethel in the *I Love Lucy* show. Being the "first" woman at a board meeting heretofore attended only by men can be unsettling.

Since I was the first woman in the college History Department where I taught at the ripe age of twenty-two, I remember a certain awkwardness in division meetings. I was new, so I stayed quiet to learn more about the culture of the institution and my division, but I felt like an outsider who did not "naturally" belong at the table. Time eased the transition for all of us. Happily, through experiences like this, most of us have learned *not* to hold people back based on traditional social norms. We have learned that a variety of people have a variety of gifts to contribute and that gifts are not distributed as one might have expected in other eras. For example, careers such as science, politics, business, the military, preaching, engineering, and construction are no longer seen as belonging only to men.

Through trial and error, as well as blood, sweat, and tears, people have learned to confirm the value of people traditionally considered so defective or "other" that they had nothing to offer or felt too alien to consider. Over time most people in the world have learned to respect the variety of humanity and to suspend judgment long enough to re-decide. Consider the contributions of Stephen Hawking, a man who might have been dismissed for his physical limitations!

One of the roles of every new generation is to challenge traditional ways. Every era and every place has blind spots due to familial, cultural, and religious traditions. Open-minded people think norms should be examined and questioned. They welcome newcomers rather than closing ranks, and they assess and reassess based on consequences and outcomes.

Change, even minor change, can be irritating when we are all settled in. Change can provoke frustration, anger, and backlash. Near the end of my teaching career I had to learn to deal with multiple gender identities. As a fan of proper English, it seemed wrong to call a single individual "they." Then I reminded myself that my students were more important than my language preferences. I needed to learn more to understand. Understanding makes us less resistant to change and more accepting of people unlike ourselves. Basically, it makes us kinder.

Although people expected thunder from the heavens in 1956, the Methodist Church and the Presbyterian Church PC (USA) granted women full clergy rights.[4] Episcopalians in the US have had women priests for over fifty years. (I remember the day of the first ordination. People expected violence, and the fire department was on call!) As ordained ministers who have both compensation and authority, women have more opportunity to enrich the work of the parishes they serve and engage people in new ways. Now we know the value of releasing the talents and insights of people who were once constrained and expected to restrain themselves and be gender appropriate. The evidence is in, so most of us have changed our minds. Given the opportunity, women have proved themselves to be as effective at leading as anyone else.

Change agents must confront the cruelties, unkindness, intolerances, and divisions of their era. Jesus would not have been crucified had he not been a reformer.[5] During the time in which he lived, blind people and lepers were considered diseased because they or their parents had sinned. Female children were a disappointment. A menstruating woman was considered "unclean." Yet at every turn Jesus displayed compassion. He taught love, forgiveness, and respect for others. He questioned practices and injustices; he broke some of the rules. He taught, often through parables and actions. He healed *on the Sabbath*. He liked to study, question, interpret,

4. Maude Jensen became the first female full clergy member of the Central Pennsylvania Conference shortly after the 1956 General Conference met. Twenty-six additional women were received as full clergy members that year.

5. Buddha and Mohammed were reformers too. What did they hope to change?

and reinterpret Scripture. He earned a reputation for challenging both religious practices and religious authorities. Yes, he was unsettling. If you scan his actions and teachings and look at his entourage of supporters, which included faithful women, it is easy to understand why he aroused fear and suspicion among both the Jewish leadership and the Roman authorities.

Some of Jesus's followers had political hopes and motives; some of them hoped he would become "king of the Jews," a title that would have raised the ire of the ruling authorities who worked for and with Rome. Jesus was executed because he and his followers were a threat to the leadership of both the Jews and the Romans. Rome's leaders wanted to destroy any political threat, and Jewish leaders wanted to suppress any religious threats. (Once again, politics and religion were involved!)

The Romans were typically tolerant of the various religions practiced in their empire if political loyalty was demonstrated. Polytheism was the norm in the classical era, so religious uniformity was not expected. Loyal citizens were expected to show respect and to pacify Rome's protective deities. Polytheistic Romans had disdain for Christians who refused to perform the simple act of dropping incense into a flame to show loyalty to the gods and to the Roman Empire. Respectfully pacifying Rome's protective deities did not seem like too much to ask. Refusing to drop the incense in the flame seemed closed minded and disloyal to the imperial government itself. In short, Roman leaders thought Christian monotheists were putting Rome at risk. Roman emperors and governors responsible for the well-being of the Roman Empire feared the spread of the Christian movement. Although typically tolerant of multiple religions, they could not allow Christian monotheism to spread lest it anger the gods.

Paul, formerly called Saul, was a classically educated Jew, a Pharisee. He was not one of the original apostles or part of Jesus's early entourage. He even took part in persecuting some of Jesus's disciples. He was on his way to do just that when he was blinded (for three days) on the road to Damascus. According to Acts 22, Jesus verbally addressed him from the heavens and asked for him to end the persecutions and play a part in spreading the Christian faith.

Paul's conversion experience led him to *change his mind*. In the 40s and 50s CE, Paul devoted himself to spreading the Christian message by traveling, preaching, and writing. His influence on Christianity was and is both profound and pervasive. Of the twenty-seven books in the New Testament, fifteen of them have been attributed to him. Scholars debate the exact number but not the weight of his influence. He was one of the early Christians who suffered execution at the hands of Rome, probably in 64–65 CE.[6]

Between the first century and the early fourth century Roman leaders sporadically persecuted Christians. The degree of persecution varied with the outlook of the various emperors and governors. Since the Romans were known to be religiously tolerant, the persecutions aroused positive and negative interest, as well as curiosity.[7] In 312, Constantine, a Roman emperor, *changed his mind* and dramatically shifted the policy of the empire. He converted to Christianity, perhaps hoping Christianity would help unite the disparate people of a divided Roman Empire.

Even though *Jesus* was one of the chosen people (the Jews), he was a compassionate man who adopted a more inclusive point of view over the course of his ministry and *changed his mind* about having a message solely for the Jews. *Paul*, a Jewish Pharisee, also *changed his mind.* After he converted to Christianity, he devoted decades of his life to spreading the Christian message throughout the Roman Empire. He was a devoted missionary until he was martyred. *Constantine changed his mind* and stopped persecuting Christians. He embraced the faith and supported it throughout the empire. Western and Eastern Europe became primarily Christian and, until 1054, more unified because of it. Take note: history unfolded in a certain way because Jesus, Paul, and Constantine *changed their minds*!

Consider what might be different if any one of the three of them had *not* changed their minds?!

Open-mindedness requires that we be less judgmental and less set in our ways. I am a historian. I have a love for the past. I also know too much fidelity to the past can become a form of idolatry. If we have too much loyalty to a particular mindset, people who disagree with us are not just wrong; they are evil. Certitude can bolster a refusal to see the need and value of change. It can also foster a furious form of piety that can be destructive. Consider the religious wars in Europe, especially in the German regions, during the seventeenth century! The Founding Fathers of the US, who were mostly practicing Christians, were also educated in the classical history of Greece and Rome, a period of diverse ideas competing for dominance, or at

6. See Koval and Asté, *Peter and Paul*, s.vv. "In the Footsteps of Paul: Saul of Tarsus: Rooted in Three Worlds."

7. Most people of the era probably thought, "Geez! Such a simple act! What's wrong with these people!"

least influence. The founders knew that to remain "united" and tolerant of diverse people and diverse beliefs, we had to have a divide between religion and politics and a tolerance of religious differences. The outcome of their efforts was the separation of church and state we have enjoyed for nearly 250 years.

Consider another turning point in history that involves someone changing his or her mind. Albert Einstein, a Jewish mathematician, fled Germany in December 1932, even though he really wanted to stay in his beloved Berlin. Hitler became chancellor of Germany in January 1933. He was a dictator by June of that year. Hitler's persecution of the Jewish people led to loss of property, imprisonment, and loss of life. Efficient death camps were established to purge Germany of Jews. Jews who recognized that such terror and persecution was ramping up were looking for a place to go.

Jewish refugees were not typically welcomed into the US, a predominately Christian nation-state, but Einstein was in demand. He had friends in Belgium (the royal family) and invitations to teach and do research at several prestigious colleges, including Oxford in Britain and Princeton in New Jersey. In 1933, four days before leaving for the US, he told an audience in England: "If you want to resist the powers which threaten to suppress intellectual and individual freedom, we must keep before us what is at stake. Without such freedom there would have been no Shakespeare, no Goethe, no Newton, no Faraday, no Pasteur, and no Lister."[8]

Einstein was reportedly drawn to the "unvarnished individuality" and "freedoms" people enjoyed in the US, and less comfortable with the "oppressive, overly refined formality" of Britain.[9] Besides, war in Europe felt close at hand in Britain. The US was safer.

Einstein was an outspoken pacifist. Pacifism was common in the interwar era because the Great War (World War I) had ground up too many soldiers and left people lame, shell shocked, blind, and wounded, emotionally and physically.[10] Einstein, like other intellectuals, including Upton Sinclair, Sigmund Freud, John Dewey, and H. G. Wells, was one of the standard-bearers of pacifist purists who thought that military training should be abolished everywhere. No armies, no war.

8. Viren, "Can Academic Freedom Survive?," 33.

9. Isaacson, *Einstein,* 396.

10. Military deaths are estimated at 8.8. million; 6 million civilians died as a direct result of WWI because of hunger, disease, and genocide. What were the reasons for the war? People still ask!

Einstein's pacifism included an aversion to nationalism and imperialism, and a call for world federalism that would protect individuals and undermine nationalistic dogmas. In 1931, he wrote: "I believe that the most important mission of the state is to protect the individual and to make it possible for him to develop into a creative personality."[11] Einstein and Freud discussed the sources of the aggressive tendency in individuals. Einstein blamed war on manipulative, ambitious leaders who stir up nationalistic passions often expressed in a military way, i.e., war. Freud argued that there is no likelihood that humanity's aggressive tendencies can be suppressed. Einstein believed that limiting the sovereignty of all nations would curtail or eliminate ambitious military action, thus creating international peace and security.[12]

Interestingly, the exchange between the two scholars was published in 1933, the same year Hitler came to power and the year that Leo Szilard, a Hungarian-German physicist working in London, conceived the idea of a nuclear "chain reaction." At that time Szilard convinced the British to make his chain reaction patent a military secret to prevent a nuclear arms race with Hitler. When scientists in Germany split the uranium atom in 1938 Szilard reversed course. He *changed his mind* about moving ahead to create an atomic weapon because he was worried that Germany might obtain an atomic bomb first. He turned his attention to building what he had hoped would never be built.

Szilard needed to convince President Roosevelt, and he thought Einstein could help with that because Einstein's reputation would carry a lot of weight. In 1939, Szilard visited Einstein and described the nuclear chain reaction concept to him. The two physicists were concerned enough about Nazi Germany creating and using such a weapon that they wrote FDR a joint letter. The letter, dated August 2, 1939, urged the president to move forward on developing an atomic bomb to thwart Hitler achieving unilateral possession of such a weapon.

Einstein had not worked on nuclear chain reaction; he was an outspoken pacifist. Even so, Szilard and two other Hungarian physicists were able to convince him that he would be particularly helpful in urging Roosevelt to move forward on developing such a weapon. Despite his personal position, Einstein decided to co-author the letter. Roosevelt wrote back to Einstein on October 19, 1939, to tell him that he was establishing a committee to

11. Isaacson, *Einstein,* 379.

12. Isaacson, *Einstein,* 382–83.

study uranium, one of the first steps in what became known as the Manhattan Project. Einstein used his influence with Roosevelt despite his pacifism, a decision that must have been difficult for him.

Einstein never worked on the Manhattan Project, and he was not made aware of plans to use atomic bombs on Hiroshima and Nagasaki in 1945. As time passed, he had regrets about his role. In 1954 he told a chemist friend of his, Linus Pauling, that the Einstein-Szilard letter was "the great mistake in my life."[13]

When new information and new challenges come about, people may have to change deeply rooted convictions to meet them. The challenges of 1939–45 looked different to Einstein in 1954. The Free World had won the war. The man who was a deep pacifist confronted real-world challenges to his values, and he regretted softening those values, even to win a war against fascism. But he did it, and it mattered. He would change his mind again.

Einstein modified his position on nationalism after the creation of Israel in 1948. *Before* the Second World War Einstein was opposed to the creation of a Jewish state, saying: "I am afraid of the inner damage Judaism will sustain—especially from the development of a narrow nationalism within our ranks. . . . The State is not in my heart."[14]

After the state of Israel was declared, Einstein wrote to a friend that he "considered the idea of a state a good one, for economic, political, and military reasons. . . . We may regret that we might have to use methods that are repulsive and stupid to us."[15] Einstein, who had once described nationalistic sentiment as divisive and dangerous, had *changed his mind*.

Using an example closer to home, imagine that a young man realizes that he is attracted to other men. The young man fears telling his parents and siblings that he is gay because he loves them and wants them in his life. He fears he will be shut out of his beloved family. A family meeting is held at which he shares his orientation and asks for their support. His father storms off, gruffly saying, "You are not my son!" Shortly thereafter the parents *changed their minds*, declared their affection for him, embraced him, and assured him that *nothing* could ever change their love for him and that they regretted their earlier reaction. They told him that his news had

13. McEvoy, "Albert Einstein's Role," para. 17.

14. Isaacson, *Einstein*, 520.

15. Isaacson, *Einstein*, 520–21.

surprised them and was not welcomed, but *he* was always welcome and would always be their much-loved son.

RELEVANT QUOTES AND TOPICS TO PONDER

- Consider this question: Have the young man's parents changed their minds or changed their hearts? Review the other examples in this chapter and experiences of your own. Do you notice a relationship between an open heart and an open mind? Give examples of your own.

"It can ruin your life only if it ruins your character. Otherwise it cannot harm you."
—Marcus Aurelius, *Meditations*

"If we've been bamboozled long enough, we tend to reject any evidence of the bamboozle. We're no longer interested in finding out the truth. The bamboozle has captured us. It's simply too painful to acknowledge, even to ourselves, that we've been taken. Once you give a charlatan power over you, you almost never get it back."
—Carl Sagan, *The Demon-Haunted World: Science as a Candle in the Dark*

"Some consider faithfulness to the gospel to mean doing what we have always done. Others find faithfulness only in being what we have always been. . . . The distinction is also essential to the understanding of discipleship in the modern church. When 'the tradition' becomes synonymous with 'the system' and maintaining the system becomes more important than maintaining the spirit of the tradition, discipleship shrivels and becomes . . . 'fidelity to the past.'"
—Sister Joan Chittister, "Living the Discipleship of Equals," address at Spirit Unbounded: Human Rights in the Emerging Catholic Church, Oct. 13, 2023

"Minds are like parachutes. They only function when they are open."
—William Rounseville Alger

"Unthinking respect for authority is the greatest enemy of truth."

—Albert Einstein, letter to Jost Winteler, 1901

"The object of opening the mind, as of opening the mouth, is to shut it again on something solid."
—G. K. Chesterton, *Week*, Sept. 27, 2024

"Do not think of knocking out another person's brains because he differs in opinion from you. It would be as rational to knock yourself on the head because you differ from yourself ten years ago."
—Horace Mann

"Nearly every revolutionary change in the history of human progress came about because someone questioned some time-honored belief or tradition and in doing so revealed a new truth, a new way of doing things, or a new standard for ethical and moral behavior. . . . A commitment to staying open and inquisitive in our own individual lives can lead us to new . . . truths that we will hopefully, for the sake of our growth, remain open to questioning."
—DailyOM, June 1, 2022

"Millenniums of brilliant minds in philosophy have not reached any one authoritative ethical system, and there is no particular reason to believe that they will ever do so."
—Rob Louis, *New York Times*, Dec. 11, 2021

"The greatest deception men suffer is from their own opinions."
—Leonardo da Vinci, *The Notebooks of Leonardo da Vinci*

Xenial (X)

Friendly, Welcoming, Kind, Understanding, Hospitable

Xenial people are curious, welcoming, and interested in understanding the people they encounter. The word "xenial" has Greek origins that reflect the Greek values of being curious about and gracious to strangers and new acquaintances. People who are inhospitable, aloof, or unfriendly are regarded as xenophobic. Xenophobic people are overly wary and/or critical of people unlike themselves, in other words, people who do not share their cultural, religious, economic, political, and/or social background. All of us find some behaviors off putting or offensive in some way, but xenophobic people often practice some form of purposeful avoidance of people unlike themselves.

A xenial person can be present to people of various kinds and cultures in a curious, nonjudgmental way. When xenial people are in a new situation or have a chance to meet new people, they are curious and try to suspend judgment and listen attentively to understand. They are friendly and open enough to put most people at ease; they experience the "otherness" of different people with a mixture of curiosity and kindness. Having once studied in Greece, I personally experienced their hospitality and generosity. (I also thought they asked a lot of questions!)

If your default way of listening is to discern what you agree or disagree with or to determine if you and the person you have just met have common ground, you are not being xenial. To relate well to someone new, listening to understand is better than passing judgment quickly to discern whether you have enough common ground with the person to invest your time and energy in the conversation. At the front end of talking to someone new, the xenial listener chooses (or decides) to *listen to understand*, not to approve or disapprove or to decide to dismiss someone or not. This personal discipline is necessary and worthwhile. If both parties can listen and suspend judgment, each person will be more at ease and posturing is less likely.

Greek culture spread throughout the Mediterranean region and into the schools and institutions the Romans built. The Romans particularly favored Stoicism, a Greek philosophy that encouraged self-discipline, duty, and the fulfillment of responsibilities typical of one's roles or position in life. Stoicism became imbedded in Roman and English legal principles and has survived to the present day.[1] Stoicism, which supports respect for everyone and their various roles in life, influenced Western ideas about human rights. Stoicism softened Roman law and the social class structure by recognizing every person and their purpose, duty, and work, as essential to the well-being of everyone else. We are all partners with various roles, and we are all necessary and to be respected because we are mutually co-dependent. External traits, like wealth and power, were tangential to one's purpose and did not negate the need and respect for each person's contribution to society. The expansion of Roman citizenship over time was in large part a by-product of these Stoic values, which the Western world inherited.[2]

Classical-era (400 BCE to 400 CE) philosophies such as Stoicism are imbedded in the culture of the Western world and are fundamental to understanding "the West." To understand the most important influences on the evolution of Western culture one would need to study the classical period and the Christian era that followed it. Classical philosophy played a part in shaping Christian theology. Saints Augustine (d. 430) and Thomas Aquinas (d. 1274) were "classically educated" intellectuals. They both played a significant role in shaping Christianity and the "Western world."[3]

Preserving and protecting the intellectual freedom to explore the big questions using human reason is a strong Western value that continues

1. The fusion of Stoicism and Roman law persists in much of Europe. English law, as practiced in Great Britain and the US, was influenced by Roman law and the idea of personal rights as well. Even so, the English legal tradition is distinct from countries with Roman law traditions. Louisiana state law has a strong French tradition, as does Quebec, a French-dominated region in Canada, so Roman law is more prominent there.

2. Law is quite evolutionary and subject to modification and reinterpretation over time. The Stoics respected the work of disciplined leaders and common people as valuable and necessary to the common good.

3. The word "theology" derives from two Greek words that mean "the study of God." Theology comes from *theos,* Greek for "God," and *-ology,* which is from the Greek word *logos,* meaning "word." Webster's Dictionary defines theology as "the rational and systematic study of religion and its influences and of the nature of religious truth." See O'Donnell, "St. Augustine"; Palmer, "Saint Thomas Aquinas."

to the present day. I would argue that the classical and Christian traditions, which evolved together, are the foundation of the Western world, "the West" as we know it today. Our cherished personal liberties have deep roots in the long evolution of Western liberalism in which classical philosophy and Christian theology played key roles. Yes, some people have been undervalued and had to wait too long, but the concept, the idea, that all human beings should have rights and options has led to a better reality for people who were once pushed to the sidelines of society.[4]

In the Free World, where religious institutions and the state are not a unified front, people have options about how they live and what they think, write, and speak. Liberty and justice for *all* is the goal of a liberal country. In the Free World, city, county, state, and federal law enforcers operate to maintain order, safety, freedom of movement, and lawful action. No religious police enforce religious rule and practices, although some secular laws and religious rules overlap ("Thou shalt not kill or steal," for example) because they are basic to good order. Thus Jewish, Buddhist, Christian, Hindu, and Muslim families, as well as nonreligious or secular families, can live side by side without holding each other in disdain or insisting that people comply with a particular religion's rules or values. In short, religious diversity creates differences, but the differences need not mean conflict. My hope is that another way to unite heterogenous individuals is the CORTHODOX Way, which offers a set of basic decency values that can give diverse people a degree of common ground.

There will always be people who think that their religion is the best and/or only way to gain God's favor. It is helpful to remember that religions are in large part human constructs that include various forms of discipline (a word related to the word "disciple") and worship. The *disciplines* of the various religions are not the thing itself, because following *rules* is not at the center of most faith traditions. Building a personal relationship with God is more often the goal. The rules and guidelines, i.e., the "dos and don'ts," simply create a fence that keeps people from veering off and becoming "lost."

4. The word "liberalism" is derived from the word "liberty." People who want to maintain or ensure personal freedom are "liberals." The ancient Greeks started the conversation and tried various forms of democracy. The Roman Republic played a role as well. Westerners learned from the Greco-Roman world and the philosophies that evolved from the classical era, especially Stoicism and the political philosophy of Aristotle. Sadly, the word 'liberal" has been used in a derogatory way in recent years. Liberals are not people for whom anything goes. They are not all similarly political minded; they do advocate and work for "liberty and justice for all."

Some religions are heavily rules centered. Some religions are relationship centered. Some religions have mystics, some do not. Some religions have both male and female leadership, some do not. The xenial approach is to seek to understand people and their culture, particularly when a specific religion has been passed along over many years and is tied into the governing system.

A xenial person sees interactions with people of different traditions as a form of exploration that enhances understanding. When Western ideas about human rights are ignored in religious states or communities, people from the Free World may feel uneasy and put off. "Freedom seeking" is one of the reasons people migrate and leave their homeland and why the West is attractive to them.

In the Free World it is morally and legally wrong to beat, maim, or kill people. Capital punishment has been abandoned or is very rare. Every person, male and female, enjoys basic human rights and the freedom to pursue their happiness.

Such liberties threaten people who would prefer to see traditional norms as ongoing and unchanging, even imposed. Other people enjoy seeking and discovering. Some people call themselves "nones" because they do not adhere to any religious tradition. Some people are Christian humanists; other people are classical humanists.[5]

In short, religious conformity is not expected in the Free World. People familiar with a variety of traditions may borrow ideas from multiple sources, combining them uniquely. Some people place the highest value on money and power. For them, life is a game at which one wins, progresses, or loses. Many Western people merge religious and secular ideologies, creating a combination of this and that. The freedom to blend, unify, and merge ideas is typical of the Western world. The humanism of the classical Greeks and Romans became the Christian humanism of the Northern Renaissance.

The lack of a state religion allows for more geniality, a warm and friendly approach. We can choose to be present and interested in others without any fear of giving up our unique identity or our own way of being. We can change our minds. We can accept the personal choices of our family, or we can embrace the ideas of other traditions. In the Free World,

5. See American Humanist Association, "Key Issues." At the heart of the various humanist movements is one question: What does a good life for human beings look like? See also American Humanist Association, "Ten Commitments."

beliefs and practices must not cause harm to others or violate the basic human decency values described in this treatise.

Most human beings are trying to lead a good life. They want similar things: reliable work, a loving family, friendships, the security and stability that come with a routine income, and the freedom to "pursue happiness." Yet many people only dream of such a life. If you live where that dream is a reality, you should know that free societies are rare, precious, and frail. Every decade, challenges emerge from self-righteous groups and their followers, both secular and religious. Freedom can certainly be messy, but it is precious and worth protecting, for everyone's sake.

People who travel and have experienced other cultures and ways of being in the world often become more xenial because they have visited places where people and their norms differ from their own, but not altogether. Family matters. Security matters. Fair play matters.

Interacting with people of all sorts leads people to seek understanding, and seeking understanding often leads to the new awareness that despite our differences we are remarkably similar creatures with a deep commonality.

The work of all human beings everywhere is to craft a life from the raw realities of birth, circumstances, and surroundings. This work can be difficult and may feel hopeless. Most people in the world have limited options and limited power, particularly people born in tyrannies or in poverty, people born female in most places of the world, and people born with disabilities. The novelist Sylvia Plath acknowledges how little latitude of free movement people have in life. She writes:

> As for free will, there is such a narrow crack of it for man to move in, crushed as he is from birth by environment, heredity, time and event and local convention.[6]

When we seek to understand another person, we are seeking to understand what that person has done with the situation they encountered because of where their "birth box" landed. We can be supportive and empathetic, especially if we have met obstacles and challenges too. We can celebrate the bright spots and successes of each other. A xenial person who enjoys advantages can indirectly experience the challenges of people who are not advantaged. We can respect each other for the obstacles we have overcome. Knowing and interacting with people from different places,

6. Popova, "Plath on Free Will," para. 5.

social classes, and a variety of situations allows people to develop strategies and coping skills and new ways to be empathetic and kind.

Many people wall themselves off from other people who cause them discomfort. It is hard to look at the despair of others and uncomfortable to come close enough to suffering to empathize without feeling overwhelmed. No wonder people of means prefer to interact with people in their social class. Very wealthy people often cocoon. They purposely eat, fly, and live apart from ordinary and less fortunate people. Sometimes the only "common" people they know work for them. Their separateness is in part a byproduct of their consumption patterns, where they dine out, where they live, how they spend money.

Sometimes people take full credit for their achievements, as if they succeeded and thrived *all* because of their own personal efforts and skills. The more accurate story of their success is that they have wisely taken advantage of the opportunities they recognized. These include access to education, a healthy body, support from a stable family, and simply where or when they were born.

Plath notes that we humans credit ourselves for our successes which we see as a function of personal excellence. Yet we attribute our failures to external circumstances. In this way of thinking, successful people often come to believe that the advantages of wealth and good fortune were all or mostly earned. This approach means that the unfortunate reap what they sow, thus ignoring the cultural, political and economic forces involved. In reality, Plath thinks our outcomes are less our doing than we imagine. She writes:

> As for free will, there is such a narrow crack of it for man to move in, crushed as he is from birth by environment, heredity, time and event and local convention. If I had been born of Italian parents in one of the caves in the hills I would be a prostitute at the age of 12 or so because I had to live (why?) and that was the only way open. If I was born into a wealthy New York family with pseudo-cultural leanings, I would have had my coming-out party along with the rest of them, and be equipped with fur coats, social contacts, and a blasé pout. How do I know? I don't; I can only guess. I wouldn't be I.[7]

Happily, some people with means and influence act rather than retreat. They are charitable, concerned, and enjoy making life better for other

7. Popova, "Plath on Free Will," para. 4.

people. They use their knowledge and money to address the large problems that hold other people back. MacKenzie Scott, Bill Gates, Melinda Gates, and Warren Buffett come to mind.[8] Jimmy Carter, whose family was well off in some ways, grew up in a humble rural region of Plains, Georgia. After his presidency, he moved back to Plains. He used his post-presidency to create the Carter Center, which has promoted democracy and peace, while working to address health issues such as Guinea worm disease. Because of the efforts of the Carter Center, Guinea worm disease could become the second human disease in history, after smallpox, to be eradicated. In short, Carter did not cocoon. He worked alongside neighbors and volunteers to build Habitat for Humanity housing. He offered a Sunday School class to whomever wished to come to his church in Plains.[9] He did not self-segregate, in part because doing so would have violated his values, which were underpinned by the Christian faith he espoused.

Like it or not, humanity is basically a large family of disparate people who are best served when people get along and work together. Competition has its place, but so do common goals, compassion, and cooperation. Xenial people choose cooperation over coercion and mutual interest over self-interest because they know that we are all in this together and that domination, which is always temporary, makes enemies, whereas partnership makes friends.

Xenial people are cordial and friendly. They seek to understand rather than to judge or exert pressure. They observe, take notice, ask friendly questions, look for common ground, and practice kindness. Xenial people work to alleviate injustices and expand opportunities for people rather than taking advantage of the weak or downtrodden. They partner more than they compete and help rather than prey on the weak. They build relationships rather than bullying people into positions or actions that they will come to resent. They are curious, caring people who do not wall themselves off.

Becoming more comfortable with a variety of people can be challenging. The Sufi tradition, an ancient spiritual discipline known as "the path of the blame," encourages people to seek out the company of people they encounter who are not like them, i.e., people they are likely to be uncomfortable around. The goal is to ultimately be able to explain and/or justify the questionable behaviors of "others."[10] Doing this requires a suspension

8. Chromy, "MacKenzie Scott Foundation."

9. Yes, I got to go several times. He was very insightful.

10. Vienne, *Art of Imperfection*, 46.

of the self and our tendency to judge people without knowing them. The goal is to seek understanding and experience empathy.

In some Native American cultures, "contrary people" behave in ways opposite of what others do. They serve as reminders that the "norms" of what is considered right are open to question.[11] By learning to recognize the difference between *being right* and *not being wrong*, we can expand our compassion, embrace our curiosity, and remain open to accepting the ways people differ from each other. Being xenial with people of all sorts allows us to push past fear of the "other" and understand more about the variety of ways people evolve into who they are. In short, a xenial outlook makes us more forgiving, more empathetic, and more helpful. When people limit themselves to their "own kind," they may become less kind to the people who are not of the same sort. They get stuck in their "ways" and become "tribal" in their point of view. Status seeking may also play a role.

Xenophobic behavior may develop in people from more isolated rural areas or closed family systems because pluralism is rarer in such communities. Thriving in rural areas is often quite challenging. A way of life develops. People are rightfully proud of their adaptability, their toughness in times of hardship, and their successes.

I grew up in Georgia and lived in medium-sized cities, but I had grandparents in rural areas. One side of my family represented the proud rural life of people who could live off the land. They farmed, hunted, fished, and gardened. I learned to drive when my feet reached the pedals of the pickup truck because my uncle let me drive in the dirt lanes the farm equipment made amid the peanut and soybean crops he planted. We listened and sang to country music ("Walkin' After Midnight" and "Everybody's Somebody's Fool"). It was rustic and *fun*. (I did not like hunting, but I did learn to shoot a rifle.)

The other side of my family was also rural. They lived about thirty-five minutes from the people I just described, yet they were quite different. They had land and farmed it using "help." They owned a small grocery store that also sold gas. They did not hunt or fish. They butchered animals and sold meat. My grandfather and uncle on my father's side were politically involved and quite at home in rural areas or in Atlanta. My grandmother had a maid most days. In short, they were refined, even proper, especially my grandmother and her daughter, my aunt. They taught my sisters and me how to set a proper table, and they warned us that no one "married well"

11. Vienne, *Art of Imperfection*, 46.

who did not develop proper speech and good manners. Until I married and invited both sides of my family to my wedding, I had no idea how uncomfortable the two sides of the family were with each other! In my eyes, they were simply different. I loved them all (well, most of them).

Perhaps being xenial requires a childlike perspective that omits judgment and enjoys the curious ways of people. It can be as simple as that. We can be like hearted even when we are not like minded. For those among us who pray and seek divine help at times, we know that God has ways of gently bringing people together who would not likely choose to be around each other. This little story serves as a reminder:

A woman locked her keys in the car and was frantic about what to do. A scruffy, rather unkempt man stopped to help. She hesitated but accepted his offer. He quickly got her on her way. She was so impressed and grateful! "Thank God!" she thought. She never knew that the man who helped her had just finished a prison sentence for stealing cars! He had recently set out to live a reformed life. It was his first act of kindness now that he had his freedom again. He felt useful. Appreciated. The encounter made him wonder, "Could I become a locksmith?"

The moral to the story is this: perhaps God often answers prayers through other people, in ways we may or may not recognize, and the interaction will typically be beneficial to both people involved. Be cautious, of course, but not too quick to reject people who seem different from you. They may be carrying gifts, and you may be too.

RELEVANT QUOTES AND TOPICS TO PONDER

"Whenever anyone asks you to ban something or hate someone, it's always worth asking, *what's in it for them?*"
—Mark Gimein, managing editor, *Week*, Feb. 17, 2023

"Even when walking in a party of no more than three I can always be certain of learning from those I am with. There will be good qualities that I can select for imitation and bad ones that will teach me what requires correction in myself."
—Confucious, "The Analects"

"Choose your leaders with wisdom and forethought.
To be led by a coward is to be controlled by all that the coward fears.

To be led by a fool is to be led by the opportunists who control the fool.
To be led by a thief is to offer up your most precious treasures to be stolen.
To be led by a liar is to ask to be told lies.
To be led by a tyrant is to sell yourself and those you love into slavery."
—Octavia E. Butler, *Parable of the Talents*

"Stop scouring people's faces for evidence that you're not enough. You will always find it because you've made that your goal."
—Brené Brown, *Braving the Wilderness: The Quest for True Belonging and the Courage to Stand Alone*

"The secret of happiness is this: let your interests be as wide as possible and let your reactions to the things and persons that interest you be as far as possible friendly rather than hostile."
—Bertrand Russell, *The Conquest of Happiness*

"The cause of *decency* is still under bombardment. . . . reasonable people remain apparently unable to exercise the kind of moral judgment and leadership that should exile extremists, frauds, and abusers from the public square—and especially from offices of public trust."
—Tom Nichols, *Atlantic Daily*, May 10, 2023

"You have your way. I have my way. As for the right way, the correct way, and the only way, it does not exist."
—Friedrich Wilhelm Nietzsche, *Thus Spoke Zarathustra*

"We have become not a melting pot but a beautiful mosaic. Different people, different beliefs, different yearnings, different hopes, different dreams. We must adjust to changing times and still hold to unchanging principles."
—Jimmy Carter

"When you're in a waiting room and an angry commentator on the corner television is telling you that the world is full of awful people who are trying to hurt you or take away what's rightfully yours, think about all the good people you know. Remember how very many good people you know and how many times a perfect stranger has been good to you in tiny ways—offering to push your cart back to the store, waving you ahead in traffic, sharing an eyeroll at the gate when yet another flight delay is announced.

"When you find yourself deeply doubting the goodness of the human race, ask yourself these questions: Who is profiting from your sadness and your anger? Who is getting rich by making you afraid? Someone is. . . .

"The world is beautiful. People are good."
—Margaret Renkl, *New York Times*, May 15, 2023

"Wisdom is the ability to see things from multiple points of view, the ability to aggregate perspectives and rest in the tensions between them."
—David Brooks, *Week*, July 26, 2024

Some of us are settled into the groups that we chose to shape our identities. That may be fine socially, but we also come together around larger causes. This example, described by Timothy Snyder, is an illustration of ordinary people coming together to exercise real change through their organizational power. He writes:

"For resistance to succeed, two boundaries must be crossed. First, ideas about change must engage people of various backgrounds who do not agree about everything. Second, people must find themselves in places that are not their homes, and among groups who were not previously their friends . . .. Nothing is real that does not end on the streets . . .. When Polish workers on the Baltic coast went on strike again in 1980, they were joined by lawyers, scholars, and others who helped them make their case. The result was a free labor union, as well as government guarantees to observe human rights. During the sixteen months that Solidarity was legal, ten million people joined, and countless new friendships were created amid strikes, marches and demonstrations. The Polish communist regime put down the movement in 1981. Yet eight years later, in 1989, when they needed negotiating partners, the communists had to turn to Solidarity. The labor union insisted on elections, which it then won. This was the beginning of the end of communism in Poland, eastern Europe, and the Soviet Union."
—Timothy Snyder, *On Tyranny: Twenty Lessons from the Twentieth Century*

"Perhaps one did not want to be loved so much as to be understood."
—George Orwell, *1984*

"We need a national narrative that points us to some ideal and gives each of us a noble role in pursuing it. That's the gigantic cultural task that lies ahead."
—David Brooks, *New York Times*, Nov. 14, 2024

"When apparent stability disintegrates,
As it must—
God is Change—
People tend to give in
To fear and depression,
To need and greed.
When no influence is strong enough
To unify people
They divide.
They struggle,
One against one,
Group against group,
For survival, position, power.
They remember old hates and generate new ones,
They create chaos and nurture it.
They kill and kill and kill,
Until they are exhausted and destroyed,
Until they are conquered by outside forces,
Or until one of them becomes
A leader
Most will follow,
Or a tyrant
Most fear.
. . . It is because we are so close to each other that our differences are so vexing. But the differences are never as great as we fancy them to be."
—Allen Dwight Callahan, Center for Action and Contemplation, Nov. 30, 2024

"America is now decades into the 'Big Sort,' the name the journalist Bill Bishop has given to the tendency of like-minded Americans to cluster

together. The dynamic is one of the dominant features of our politics and our culture. White, rural America is very, very red. Diverse, urban America is very, very blue. . . . The result is a series of starkly different experiences for different American populations that directly depends on whether you're an outsider or an insider."
—David French, *New York Times*, July 27, 2023

"Most people—maybe more than you think—are peace- and love-seeking creatures who are sometimes caught in bad situations. The most practical thing you can do, even in hard times, is to lead with curiosity, lead with respect, work to understand the people you might be taught to detest. That means seeing people with generous eyes, offering trust to others before they trust you. That means adopting a certain posture toward the world. If you look at others with the eyes of fear and judgment, you will find flaws and menace; but if you look out with a respectful attitude, you'll often find imperfect people enmeshed in uncertainty, doing the best they can."
—David Brooks, *New York Times*, Nov. 5, 2021

"I'm not in this world to live up to your expectations and you're not in this world to live up to mine."
—Bruce Lee

"Let there be no compulsion in religion." (2:257)
"Unto you your religion, and unto me my religion." (109:6)
—Muhammad, Qur'an

- If everyone in an imaginary country believes that a moral code should be enforced by the state, is it then "democratic" and therefore "good"? Is agreement by the many the *source* of the highest law? What else might be?
- With regard to abortion, in what way should abortion laws be decided in a free or liberal society? What is the role of science? What is the role of belief systems?
- Discuss ways in which "the people" can act to shut down or at least not reward indecent behaviors while maintaining open-minded acceptance of diverse ways of being together?

- Debate whether the name-calling practice of "wokeness" has a positive or negative effect, socially and politically. Is this a forced "either/or"? What is the outcome of dividing people into these two groups? What are the criteria for belonging to the woke? The unwoke?

- People who practice "honor violence" may consider themselves virtuous for enforcing a moral religious code that developed over a thousand years ago in migratory societies that for practical reasons did not have a functioning judicial system. In liberal/pluralistic societies, religious freedom does not include the right to physically harm another person. Consider this:

  A Pakistani man in Brooklyn, New York, beat his wife to death with a stick because she made him a meal of lentils rather than the goat meat he had requested. His defense attorney opened his argument in court by saying the defendant "believed" he had the right to hit and discipline his wife and that the defendant had not *meant* to kill her. He also argued that prison would be a hardship for the defendant because the man would not have access to Pakistani food.[12]

  What would you do if you were the judge? What role does "belief," religious or otherwise, play in deciding moral or immoral actions? Does it matter that the defendant said he did not mean to kill her?

- Use this link to make observations about the various levels of freedom around the world: https://worldpopulationreview.com/countryrankings/freestcountries.

  Notice which countries rank in the top ten list of countries living in freedom. How many are Western countries or have a historic connection to one or more Western liberal countries? To countries in the East? The South? About the bottom 10 countries, where freedom is quite limited, what factors affect their low ranking?

  At the time of this writing, the US scored 83 out of 100 on this ranking (as did Romania, Croatia, South Korea, and Panama) and was ranked 58 out of 193 countries. What explains that rating?

  What are the top ten countries on the index? What explains that rating? How do you anticipate these rankings will change?

  Compare (similarities) and contrast (differences) two countries, one that has a high rating and one that has a low rating. Explain reasons for the ratings and the odds or opportunities for those ratings changing over time.

12. Yaniv, "Pakistani Man"; Associated Press, "Man, 75, Kills Wife."

Final Note

In 1959 the British jurist Patrick Devlin made a point that should haunt us: "Without shared ideas on politics, morals and ethics, no society can exist."[1] Perhaps we can begin by advocating, practicing, and expecting basic decency from each other.

If you decide to embrace the CORTHODOX decency values, you will be applying the nine fundamental values discussed here to ordinary situations that are part of your daily life. As a result, you will be doing your part as a personal example of decent behaviors and as a person partially responsible for social cohesion. As W. L. Sheldon wrote: "There is nothing noble in being superior to your fellow man; true nobility is being superior to your former self."[2]

To apply these decency norms to specific situations and individual circumstances requires both the awareness of the value of the norms described *and* practice, daily practice. In your own way and in your own setting, try to live and represent these decency norms and help them become "normal." Post the chart on the next page in multiple places to remind yourself, and you will remind other people too. Every one of us has a circle of influence. Think about how the CORTHODOX Way can be explored and used in your personal settings. We are all being watched. We are all ambassadors of some sort.

My wish for you, dear reader, is that you enjoy "the art of living well." This phrase, which belonged to the classical Greeks and the Renaissance humanists, can have a variety of interpretations. The CORTHODOX decency values offer an approach and an opportunity.

1. Eckman, "Thinking Critically"; *New York Times*, "Getting the Election Wrong."
2. Vermillion, "Most Famous Things," quote 5.

Under the guidance of a mature conscience, intentional awareness, and self-discipline, you can live the "good life," a life as unique to you as your circumstances, challenges, and opportunities, and a life that serves as an example to other people as well.

—On Decency—

The CORTHODOX Way

Compassionate (Empathetic, Charitable, Kind)

Objective (Rational, Unbiased, Curious)

Responsible (Accountable, Deliberate)

Trustworthy (Reliable, Honest, Truthful)

Humble (Grateful, Forgiving of Self and Others)

Original (Creative, Assertive, Contributes)

Disciplined (Persistent, Centered, Hopeful)

Open Minded (Listens, Questions, Changes)

Xenial (Friendly, Understanding, Welcoming)

Bibliography

The 1619 Project. https://www.nytimes.com/interactive/2019/08/14/magazine/1619-america-slavery.html.

ABC News. "'Born in Kenya': Obama's Literary Agent Misidentified His Birthplace in 1991." ABC News, May 17, 2012. https://abcnews.go.com/Politics/OTUS/born-kenya-obamas-literary-agent-misidentified-birthplace-1991/story?id=16372566.

Alberta, Tim. "The Senator Who Decided to Tell the Truth." *Atlantic*, June 30, 2021. https://www.theatlantic.com/politics/archive/2021/06/michigan-republican-truth-election-fraud/619326/.

American Humanist Association. "Key Issues." American Humanist Association, n.d. https://americanhumanist.org/key-issues/.

———. "Ten Commitments." American Humanist Association, n.d. https://americanhumanistcenterforeducation.org/ten-commitments/.

American Rhetoric. "McCarthy-Welch Exchange: 'Have You Left No Sense of Decency?'" American Rhetoric, last updated Dec. 24, 2020. From June 9, 1954, during the Army-McCarthy hearings in Washington, DC. https://www.americanrhetoric.com/speeches/welch-mccarthy.html.

Associated Press. "Man, 75, Kills Wife Because She Served Him Lentils for Dinner: Prosecutor." NBC New York, May 22, 2014. https://www.nbcnewyork.com/news/local/man-kills-wife-wrong-meal-lentil-goat-arrest-court-prosecutor/2002485/.

Atwood, Margaret. *The Handmaid's Tale*. Boston: Houghton Mifflin, 1986.

Biblical Hermeneutics. "What Did Jesus Mean When He Said, Forgive Them 'for They Know Not What They Do'?" Biblical Hermeneutics, 2017; last updated 2024. https://hermeneutics.stackexchange.com/questions/29423/what-did-jesus-mean-when-he-said-forgive-them-for-they-know-not-what-they-do.

Bradley, John P., et al., eds. *The International Dictionary of Thoughts from Ancient, Medieval, Modern and Contemporary Times*. Chicago: Ferguson, 1975

Brinkhof, Tim. "'Have You No Sense of Decency?' The Question That Took Down Senator Joe McCarthy." Mental Floss, May 13, 2024. https://www.mentalfloss.com/posts/have-you-no-decency-quote.

Brooks, Arthur C. "Fyodor Dostoyevsky's Five Principles of Personal Freedom." *Atlantic*, July 25, 2024. https://www.theatlantic.com/ideas/archive/2024/07/fyodor-dostoyevsky-formula-happiness/679203/.

Brooks, David. "At His Core." *New York Times*, Oct. 21, 2020.

———. "The Culture Wars Have Gone Global." *New York Times*, Apr. 10, 2020.

———. "A Surprising Route to the Best Life Possible." *New York Times*, Mar. 27, 2025.

Brown, Brené. *Daring Greatly*. New York: Avery, 2012.

Bruni, Frank. "The Most Important Thing I Teach My Students Isn't on the Syllabus." *New York Times*, Apr. 20, 2024. https://www.nytimes.com/2024/04/20/opinion/students-humility-american-politics.html.

Center for Contemplative Science and Compassion-Based Ethics. "Overview of CBCT." CCSCBE, n.d. https://compassion.emory.edu/cbct-compassion-training/index.html.

Chen, Joyce. "12 Quotes to Help You Let Go of Bitterness." Inspiring Quotes, June 13, 2023. https://inspiringquotes.com/12-quotes-to-help-you-let-go-of-bitterness/.

Christian Nationalism Research. https://prri.org/prri-research/prri-issues/christian-nationalism/.

Chromy, Melaina. "MacKenzie Scott Foundation & Grant Explained." Bloomerang, last updated Sept. 16, 2025. https://bloomerang.com/blog/mackenzie-scott-foundation-grant-guide/.

Coleman, Alistair. "Chemtrails: What's the Truth Behind the Conspiracy Theory?" BBC News, July 23, 2022. https://www.bbc.com/news/blogs-trending-62240071.amp.

Colón, Suzan. "Seven Heavenly Virtues." *Britannica*, June 27, 2025. https://www.britannica.com/topic/seven-heavenly-virtues.

Defense Casualty Analysis System. "World War II." DCAS, n.d. https://dcas.dmdc.osd.mil/dcas/app/conflictCasualties/ww2.

De Mello, Anthony. *One Minute Wisdom*. New York: Image Doubleday, 1985.

Democracy Now! "'Where's My Roy Cohn?' Film Explores How Joseph McCarthy's Ex-Aide Mentored Trump & Roger Stone." YouTube, Jan. 28, 2019. https://www.youtube.com/watch?v=t9f8x999cUw.

Douthat, Ross. "We Aren't in Vegas Anymore." *New York Times*, Feb. 13, 2022.

Duda, Dan. "One with Everything?" Seti League, last updated Feb. 6, 2016. From *Penn Central* (Dec. 2015). https://www.setileague.org/editor/zen.htm.

Eagleman, David, host. *The Brain*. Episode 3, clip 1, "Ian Waterman's Inspiring Story." Aired Oct. 28, 2015, on PBS. https://www.pbs.org/video/brain-david-eagleman-episode-3-clip-1/.

Eckman, Jim. "Thinking Critically and Biblically About Identity Politics and the D.E.I Monoculture." Issues in Perspective, Jan. 4, 2025. https://issuesinperspective.com/2025/01/thinking-critically-and-biblically-about-identity-politics-and-the-d-e-i-monoculture/.

Encyclopedia of Mental Disorders. "Hare Psychopathy Checklist." *Encyclopedia of Mental Disorders*, n.d. http://www.minddisorders.com/Flu-Inv/Hare-Psychopathy-Checklist.html#google_vignette.

Falk, William. "Editor's Letter." *Week* (June 3, 2022) 3. https://www.zinio.com/article/the-week-magazine/june-3-2022-1538355/editors-letter-ao.

Fournier, Tom. "The Ancient Virtue Antidote." *Mensa Bulletin* (Feb. 2022) 29.

French, David. "The Truth About Extremism That American Likes to Forget." *Atlantic*, May 19, 2022. https://www.theatlantic.com/newsletters/archive/2022/05/buffalo-shooting-manifesto-extremism-great-replacement/676566/.

Frenkel, Sheera, and Cecilia Kang. *An Ugly Truth: Inside Facebook's Battle for Domination*. New York: Harper, 2021.

Fritzsche, Peter. "Hitler and the Holocaust." *New York Times*, Aug. 28, 2020. https://www.nytimes.com/2020/08/28/books/review/volker-ullrich-hitler-downfall-1939-1944.html.

Fuller, Heather. "The 'Unbroken' Story Changes Today's Challenged Teens into World-Changers." Louis Zamperini Foundation, Sept. 29, 2018. From *Christian Post*. https://www.zamperini.org/news/2018/9/29/op-ed-as-published-in-the-christian-post.

Gandhi, Mahatma. "The Gita and Satyagraha: The Philosophy of Non-Violence and the Doctrine of the Sword: A Letter from Tolstoy to Gandhi." Mahatma Gandhi, 1910, 1936. Russian translated by Pauline Padlashuk. https://www.mkgandhi.org/swmgandhi/chap02.php.

Garber, Megan. "We've Lost the Plot." *Atlantic*, Jan. 30, 2023; last updated May 10, 2023. https://www.theatlantic.com/magazine/archive/2023/03/tv-politics-entertainment-metaverse/672773/.

Gettysburg College. "What Is Hinduism?" Gettysburg College, n.d. https://www.gettysburg.edu/offices/religious-spiritual-life/world-religions-101/what-is-hinduism.

Goldberg, Jeffrey. "The Media Challenge Before Us." *Atlantic Magazine* (Oct. 2023) 10.

Golden, Bernard. "Displaced Anger: One Destructive Way We Disavow Anger." *Psychology Today*, July 23, 2020. https://www.psychologytoday.com/us/blog/overcoming-destructive-anger/202007/displaced-anger-one-destructive-way-we-disavow-anger.

Greenfieldboyce, Nell. "Why Some Astronomers Once Feared NASA's James Webb Space Telescope Would Never Launch." NPR, Dec. 22, 2021. https://www.npr.org/2021/12/22/1066377182/why-some-astronomers-once-feared-nasas-james-webb-space-telescope-would-never-la.

Gross, Terry. "Reporters Reveal 'Ugly Truth' of How Facebook Enables Hate Groups and Disinformation." NPR, July 13, 2021. https://www.npr.org/2021/07/13/1015483097/an-ugly-truth-how-facebook-enables-hate-and-disinformation.

Higgins, Isabella. "British Prime Minister Boris Johnson Opens COP26 Climate Conference with Dire Warning." ABC, Nov. 1, 2021. https://www.abc.net.au/news/2021-11-02/boris-johnson-warns-climate-summit-doomsday-approaching/100586720.

History.com Editors. ""Have You No Sense of Decency?' Sen. Joseph McCarthy Is Asked in Hearing." History, Nov. 13, 2009; last updated May 28, 2025. https://www.history.com/this-day-in-history/june-9/joseph-mccarthy-meets-his-match.

Howard, Lisa. *Stop Manipulating Me! Identifying Narcissism, Disarming a Narcissist & Overcoming Narcissistic Abuse*. Self-published, 2019.

Irvine, William B. *A Guide to the Good Life: The Ancient Art of Stoic Joy*. Oxford: Oxford University Press, 2009.

Isaacson, Walter. *Einstein: His Life and Universe*. New York: Simon and Schuster, 2007.

Jane Goodall Institute. "Environmental Icon Dr. Jane Goodall to Celebrate 90th Birthday Year Spreading a Message of 'Hope Through Action' Across the Globe." Jane Goodall Institute, Feb. 2, 2024. https://janegoodall.org/environmental-icon-dr-jane-goodall-to-celebrate-90th-birthday-year-spreading-a-message-of-hope-through-action-across-the-globe/.

Jazaieri, Hooria, et al. "Enhancing Compassion: A Randomized Controlled Trial of a Compassion Cultivation Training Program." *Journal of Happiness Studies* 14 (2013) 1113–26. https://doi.org/10.1007/s10902-012-9373-z.

Johnson, Lennox. "He who knows only his own side of the case, knows little of that"—a Classic Reading from *On Liberty* by John Stuart Mill." Daily Idea, Dec. 15, 2020. https://thedailyidea.org/own-side-of-the-case-on-liberty-john-stuart-mill/.

Johnson, Steven. "The Living Century." *New York Times Magazine* (May 2, 2021) 12–21, 54–61.

Kari, Daven M. “Evelyn Underhill.” EBSCO, 2023. https://www.ebsco.com/research-starters/biography/evelyn-underhill.

Keith, Kent. “Mensa Brain or Monkey Brain? Which Is at the Helm of Our Voluntary Activities?” *Mensa Bulletin* (Apr./May 2021) 29–32.

Klein, Ezra. “The Chief Ideologist of the Silicon Valley Elite Has Some Strange Ideas.” *New York Times*, Oct. 26, 2023. https://www.nytimes.com/2023/10/26/opinion/marc-andreessen-reactionary-futurism.html.

———. “The Rise of Reactionary Futurism.” *New York Times*, Oct. 29, 2023.

Kleuk, Garrison “Bud.” “Righteous Indignation and Porn.” *Mensa Bulletin* (Feb. 2021) 18.

Koval, Margaret, and Patricia Asté. *Peter and Paul and the Christian Revolution*. Aired Apr. 2003 on PBS. https://www.pbs.org/empires/peterandpaul/footsteps/footsteps_1_1.html.

LaFrance, Adrienne. “The New Anarchy.” *Atlantic* (Apr. 2023) 22–37.

Lam, Raymond. “Being Humble Is Itself a Spiritual Practice.” Buddhistdoor Global, July 25, 2010. https://www.buddhistdoor.net/features/being-humble-is-itself-a-spiritual-practice/.

Lewis, C. S. *The Screwtape Letters*. New York: MacMillan, 1961.

Lewis, Jacqui. *Courage and Rule-Breaking Kindness That Can Heal the World*. New York: Harmony/Penguin Random House, 2021.

Maiden, John. “What Is the New Apostolic Reformation (NAR)?” *Premier Christianity*, Nov. 6, 2023. https://www.premierchristianity.com/what-is-the-new-apostolic-reformation-nar/16665.article.

Mayo Clinic Staff. “Debunking COVID-19 Myths.” Mayo Clinic, Sept. 7, 2024. https://www.mayoclinic.org/diseases-conditions/coronavirus/in-depth/coronavirus-myths/art-20485720.

McCrummen, Stephanie. “Warrior for the . . . Future.” *Week* (July 22, 2022) 40.

McEvoy, Colin. “Albert Einstein’s Role in the Atomic Bomb Was the ‘One Great Mistake in My Life.’” Biography, last updated Jan. 7, 2024. https://www.biography.com/scientists/a44402742/albert-einstein-role-in-the-atomic-bomb.

McLaren, Brian D. “Love Is Stronger Than Hope.” Center for Action and Contemplation, May 14, 2024. https://cac.org/daily-meditations/love-is-stronger-than-hope/.

———. *A New Kind of Christian: A Tale of Two Friends on a Spiritual Journey*. San Francisco: Jossey-Bass, 2001.

McSorley, Jeanne. “The Codes That Guide Our Lives.” *New York Times*, Apr. 11, 2021.

Mill, John Stuart. “Of the Liberty of Thought and Discussion.” College Sidekick, n.d. From *On Liberty*, ch. 2. https://courses.lumenlearning.com/sanjacinto-philosophy/chapter/john-stuart-mill-on-liberty-chapter-2-of-the-liberty-of-thought-and-discussion/.

Miller, Phyllis Zimbler. “1933 Germany’s Democracy Legally Dismantled in 53 Days.” Miller Mosaic, Jan. 17, 2025. https://www.millermosaicllc.com/1933-germanys-democracy-legally-dismantled-in-53-days/.

Moynihan, Daniel. “No Easy Answers.” *New York Times*, June 4, 2021.

National WWII Museum. “Research Starters: Worldwide Deaths in World War II.” National WWII Museum, n.d. https://www.nationalww2museum.org/students-teachers/student-resources/research-starters/research-starters-worldwide-deaths-world-war.

New York Times. “Getting the Election Wrong, and Right.” *New York Times*, Nov. 24, 2024. https://www.nytimes.com/2024/11/24/opinion/trump-harris-election-lessons.html.

O'Brien, Barbara. "Christian Nationalism: Power, Politics, and a Distorted Gospel." Religious History Nerd, last updated June 2, 2025. https://www.patheos.com/blogs/thereligioushistorynerd/2022/10/a-brief-history-of-christian-nationalism-from-the-founders-to-the-cold-war/.

———. "The Principle of Dependent Origination in Buddhism." Learn Religions, last updated June 25, 2019. https://www.learnreligions.com/dependent-origination-meaning-449723.

O'Donnell, James. "St. Augustine." *Britannica*, July 20, 1998; last updated Oct. 18, 2025. https://www.britannica.com/biography/Saint-Augustine.

Paine, Herb. "The Intellectual Divide." *Mensa Bulletin* (Jan. 2025) 32–37.

Palmer, Stone. "Saint Thomas Aquinas." Biography Host, Feb. 3, 2025. https://biographyhost.com/p/saint-thomas-aquinas-biography.html.

Patenaude, Bertrand M. "Regional Perspectives on Human Rights: The USSR and Russia, Part One." Stanford Program on International and Cross-Cultural Education, Fall 2012. https://spice.fsi.stanford.edu/docs/regional_perspectives_on_human_rights_the_ussr_and_russia_part_one.

Paul, Richard, and Linda Elder. *The Miniature Guide to Critical Thinking: Concepts and Tools*. Thinker's Guide Library. Tomales, CA: Foundation for Critical Thinking, 2003.

PBS *News Hour*. "The 1619 Project Details the Legacy of Slavery in America." PBS *News Hour*, Aug. 18, 2019. https://www.pbs.org/newshour/show/the-1619-project-details-the-legacy-of-slavery-in-america.

Peck, M. Scott. *People of the Lie: The Hope for Healing Human Evil*. New York: Simon and Schuster, 1983.

Peters, Jeremy W. "One Republican's Lonely Fight Against a Flood of Disinformation." *New York Times*, Apr. 3, 2021. https://www.nytimes.com/2021/04/03/us/politics/denver-riggleman-republican-disinformation.html.

Plath, Sylvia. *The Unabridged Journals of Sylvia Plath: Transcripts from the Original Manuscripts at Smith College*. Edited by Karen V. Kukil. New York: Knopf, 2000.

Popova, Maria. "The Stoic Key to Kindness." *Marginalian*, June 1, 2022. https://www.themarginalian.org/2022/06/01/marcus-aurelius-meditations-kindness.

———. "Sylvia Plath on Free Will, the Pillars of Personhood, and What Makes Us Who We Are." *Marginalian*, July 31, 2022. https://www.themarginalian.org/2015/10/27/sylvia-plath-journals-privilege-free-will.

———. "William James on Choosing Purpose over Profit and the Life-Changing Power of a Great Mentor." *Marginalian*, Oct. 31, 2014. https://www.themarginalian.org/2014/10/31/william-james-profit-purpose.

Psychology Today Staff. "Assertiveness." *Psychology Today*, n.d. https://www.psychologytoday.com/us/basics/assertiveness.

Reis, Gilmar, et al. "Effect of Early Treatment with Ivermectin Among Patients with Covid-19." *New England Journal of Medicine* 386 (2022) 1721–31. https://www.nejm.org/doi/full/10.1056/NEJMoa2115869.

Reuters Fact Check. "Fact Check: Does '2000 Mules' Provide Evidence of Voter Fraud in the 2020 U.S. Presidential Election?" *Reuters*, May 27, 2022. https://www.reuters.com/article/fact-check/does-2000-mules-provide-evidence-of-voter-fraud-in-the-2020-us-presidential-idUSL2N2XJ0OQ/.

Rhoades, Tracey. "35 Elie Wiesel Quotes About Hope, Injustice and Gratitude." *Parade*, Apr. 20, 2024. https://parade.com/living/elie-wiesel-quotes.

Romey, Linda. "Brothers and Sisters in Humanity." *Mount Magazine* [Benedictine Sisters of Erie] 34 (2021) 10–11.

Roos, Dave. "What Are the 8 Beatitudes, and What Do They Mean?" *How Stuff Works*, last updated June 7, 2024. https://people.howstuffworks.com/beatitudes.htm.

Schwartz, Mattathias. "The Advocate." *New York Times Magazine*, June 7, 2020.

Slezkine, Peter. "What Happened to the 'Free World'?" *New Republic*, May 22, 2018. https://newrepublic.com/article/148479/happened-free-world.

Smarsh, Sarah. "What to Do with Our Covid Rage." *New York Times*, Aug. 8, 2021.

Snelling, John. *The Buddhist Handbook: The Complete Guide to Buddhist Schools, Teaching, Practice, and History*. Rochester, VT: Inner Traditions, 1998.

Spring, Marianna. "US Election 2020: 'QAnon Might Affect How My Friends Vote.'" BBC, Oct. 10, 2020. https://www.bbc.com/news/blogs-trending-54440973.

St. George, Zach. "The Long Tale: Mainstream Science Has Tried Its Best to Debunk a Theory That Says a Comet Struck Earth 13,000 Years Ago." *New York Times Magazine* (Mar. 3, 2024) 30–35, 45.

Swanson, Kenneth. *Enter the Kingdom: Embracing Christian Virtue*. Eugene, OR: Wipf & Stock, 2024.

Tarnaff, Ben. "What Would a More Egalitarian Internet Look Like?" *New York Times*, May 29, 2022.

Telushkin, Joseph. "Charity (Tzedekah): What Is Tzedekah?" Jewish Virtual Library, 1991. From *Jewish Literacy* (New York: Morrow and Co.). https://www.jewishvirtuallibrary.org/what-is-tzedakah.

Thompson, Derek. "Why Are We Still Arguing About Masks?" *Atlantic*, Mar. 3, 2023. https://www.theatlantic.com/newsletters/archive/2023/03/covid-lab-leak-mask-mandates-science-media-information/673263/.

Tomlin, E. W. F. *The Great Philosophers of the Western World*. New York: Wyn, 1952.

United Nations. "Universal Declaration of Human Rights." United Nations, Dec. 10, 1948. https://www.un.org/en/about-us/universal-declaration-of-human-rights.

Van Marrewijk, Lisanne. "The 3 Elements of Self-Compassion, According to Kristin Neff." Self-Compassion Academy, Feb. 21, 2025. https://selfcompassionacademy.com/kristin-neff-self-compassion/.

Vermillion, Stephanie. "The Most Famous Things Ernest Hemingway Never Said." Inspiring Quotes, Mar. 18, 2021. https://inspiringquotes.com/the-most-famous-things-ernest-hemingway-never-said/.

Vienne, Veronique. *The Art of Imperfection: Simple Ways to Make Peace With Yourself*. New York: Clarkson Potter, 1999.

Viren, Sarah. "Can Academic Freedom Survive?" *New York Times Magazine* (June 6, 2025) 30–49. https://www.nytimes.com/issue/magazine/2025/06/06/the-6082025-issue.

Week. "Fox: A Culture of Lying Exposed." (Dec. 31, 2021/Jan. 7, 2022) 19.

———. "Wit and Wisdom." *Week* (Feb. 16, 2024) 17.

Wertheimer, Linda. "Fake News Surge Pins D.C. Pizzeria As Home to Child-Trafficking." NPR, Nov. 27, 2016. https://www.npr.org/2016/11/27/503489400/fake-news-surge-pins-d-c-pizzeria-as-home-to-child-trafficking.

Yang-Ming, Wang. "Inquiry on the Great Learning." In *Classics of Eastern Thought*, edited by Lynn H. Nelson and Patrick Peebles, 301–5. New York: Harcourt Brace College, 1991.

Yaniv, Oren. "Pakistani Man Gets 18 Years to Life for Beating Wife to Death After She Made Lentils for Dinner." *New York Daily News*, July 9, 2014; updated Jan. 9, 2019.

https://www.nydailynews.com/2014/07/09/pakistani-man-gets-18-years-to-life-for-beating-wife-to-death-after-she-made-lentils-for-dinner/.
Zinnemann, Fred, dir. *A Man for All Seasons*. Los Angeles: Columbia, 1966.
Zuboff, Shoshanna. *The Age of Surveillance Capitalism: The Fight for a Human Future at the New Frontier of Power*. New York: Public Affairs, 2018.
———. "You Are the Object of a Secret Extraction Operation." *New York Times*, Nov. 12, 2021. https://www.nytimes.com/2021/11/12/opinion/facebook-privacy.html.
Zwelling, Leonard. "Humility Is the Antidote to Grievance." Lew Zwelling, May 10, 2024. https://lenzwelling.com/2024/05/humility-is-the-antidote-to-grievance/.

www.ingramcontent.com/pod-product-compliance
Lightning Source LLC
LaVergne TN
LVHW020632100826
845148LV00012B/2154

9798385263004